AMERICAN
GOVERNMENT:

AMERICAN GOVERNMENT:

WELCOME TO THE MODERATE PARTY

CHARLES BINGMAN

AMERICAN GOVERNMENT:
WELCOME TO THE MODERATE PARTY

iUniverse books may be ordered through booksellers or by contacting:

iUniverse
1663 Liberty Drive
Bloomington, IN 47403
www.iuniverse.com
1-800-Authors (1-800-288-4677)

ISBN: 978-1-5320-8189-7 (sc)
ISBN: 978-1-5320-8190-3 (e)

Library of Congress Control Number: 2019913151

Print information available on the last page.

iUniverse rev. date: 09/06/2019

CONTENTS

INTRODUCTION

The world is changing – but of course, it has always been changing. Gone are the horse and carriage, and in have come the horseless carriages by the hundreds of millions. Gone are the canals, and in are super highways. Education no longer peaks at the 6th grade or the 12th grade but at the post-doctoral level. The wood stove has become the home heating/cooling system. The ice box is out, and the refrigerator is in, and full up.

"Governance" is a far broader concept than just the governments themselves since it encompasses the involvement of individuals and orgnizations in some form in the affairs of governments. Governance includes the roles of corporations, interest groups and non-government institutions as well. The whole thing starts with a great debate: what is it the government is really supposed to do?

In the past, the answer has ranged from "nothing" to "everything"; from letting the peasants starve, to government "from the cradle to the grave". By UN definition, there are 196 countries in the world. Perhaps 40-50 of them are very small, or remote islands, important for those living there, but not weighty in world affairs. There are thus about 150 substantial governments, and all of them without exception are run from the top down by centrist elites, and about 105 of them are in deep trouble. "Deep trouble" is defined as involving wars, insurrections, serious internal conflict, deliberate skewing of wealth, lack of social justice, and lack of social services and public infrastructure. Most of these governments suffer from poor management, bumbling incompetence and rampant corruption. Most of them suffer from problems created and extended by the governments themselves out of motives of greed, viciousness and an insatiable lust for power.

In its totality, the American national governance system is unbelievably huge and complex, sophisticated, complicated, muddled and notoriously fragmented and yet interrelated. It is probably unwise to think of it as "the government" since it is literally hundreds of governments, program by program and place by place. In short, it has never been a coherent entity designed to be "managed" as that term is understood in other contexts. The best way to evaluate government is first from the top down, and second from the middle down. From the top down, governments are created and designed not for management effectiveness but for political interpretations, and the political view of the world is often markedly different from the professional management view. Thus, public managers are faced with conditions far different and far more complicated than those face by the executives and managers in the private sector.

The President is, by order of the Constitution, the Chief Executive of the government, and yet not even the President can really manage the totality the way chief executives of corporations can manage. Much of the operational power and authority for specific government programs is vested by law not in the President but in the head of the government agency that delivers the program. Cabinet secretaries and agency heads may "work for" the President and be appointed by him, but each also "works for" the Congress which defines his or her programs, dictates agency structure, defines many of its processes, and ultimately controls its finances. The President cannot order his leaders to violate the law, and should be careful not to try.

The U. S. became an economic powerhouse through the world's finest manufacturing capacity. But manufacturing has gradually been overtaken by its own success because it financed the surge of the consumer economy that dominates the economic horizon today. More and more of the total economy is commercial, including banking and insurance, higher education, government, and millions of jobs in offices, retail establishments and "brain" occupations. The picks and shovels have largely been replaced by the telephone and the computer.

More and more, the future has become the cities. In 1930, 60% of the U. S. population lived on farms and in rural communities and small towns. Today, that number is down to about 15%. The world is awakening to the fact that the future will be increasingly urban, and neither central governments nor cities themselves seem fully ready to cope. Many of the world's largest cities are already overwhelmed. All over the world, massive shifts of population are occurring from rural and village life to urban life. This movement has been largely stabilized in the most developed countries, but in the less developed countries, a serious decline of primary level jobs (i.e. agriculture, mining, forestry, and fishing) is taking place because of the low economic value derived from these occupations, and this decline is forcing millions to move to cities in the hope of finding a better livelihood. This movement is spontaneous and irreversible. This creates two kinds of problems: first, the overburden and potential collapse of urban economies and infrastructure; and second, the decline of rural society, despite efforts of many countries to subsidize and prop up rural economies and enhance rural development.

The huge surge of people to cities has meant that especially the largest and most densely populated cities has dramatically increased the need for high quality public infrastructure which has risen in importance. As cities fall behind the power curve, it has become harder and harder to catch up again. When nations fail and collapse, the process of disintegration mutilates institutions and destroys the underlying understandings between the government and the governed. This is precisely why state rebuilding must be sustained, and requires time, massive capacity building, large sums from the outside, debt relief, and appropriate forms of tutoring. But note: not even the U. N. or the U. S. can be held responsible for rebuilding other governments around the world. Many humanitarian voices advocate exactly that, but the only way to resurrect more than a hundred failed or floundering states is for each to remain responsible for its own fate.

The whole world including the United States is experiencing a huge surge in population. Almost every sector of economy is becoming more sophisticated and more productive, and despite the most ominous of predictions, the world has almost never run out of critical resources. There have been major improvements, worldwide, in technology, education, the body of usable knowledge, in managerial skills, and in the value-added nature of economic sectors. There is less reliance on primary economic sectors (farming, fishing, mining, forestry) and a movement upscale to more value added secondary and tertiary levels of economic activity. Here are some of the most important ways in which the world has become better:

1. Transportation: air travel has grown beyond belief; hundreds of millions of people now have their own automobiles; thousands of miles of highways and urban streets have been provided; the number of air line passengers is simply staggering; and in all modes, the cost per unit mile of travel is, remarkably, down.

2. Despite repeated ominous predictions of world wide starvation, food is far more widely available. New techniques, better farming equipment, new fertilizers and insecticides have allowed far greater

production on far frewer acres under cultivation. Food is available in remarkable variation at far more affordable cost.

3.   The expected life span of humans in 1900 was 41. In 1930, it was 59. In 2000, it was 77, and it is close to 80 now.

4.   Millions of women have entered the workforce. In 2015, 74% of working age women were in the labor force, compared to about 35% in 1946. In addition, the value of jobs held by women is uniformly higher and more productive.

5.   Almost all forms of medicine are unbelievably advanced. Most of the horrible diseases of the past – plagues, small pox, measles, polio, influenza have largely been eliminated. New problems such as obesity, drug addition and AIDS are being dealt with as individual problems.

6.   Humans are more willing and able to move to improve their lives. Immigration and emmigration, while difficult in the short run, prove to be invaluable in the longer term. The tragedy is the fact that "mobiliity" is now so often the fate of refugees and displaced persons, but there is a substantial record of humane efforts to deal with these problems.

7.   Machines that replace human labor have multiplied, and greatly reduced the cost of producing most "things". Machines have enabled the greater expansion of economies, creating more wealth and new forms of work.

8.   Communications have experienced a remarkable revolution, especially in the form of computers and cell phones, and the world of the average person will never be the same – but usually better.

9.   Home ownership is much more likely, and homes are totally better and more convenient: heating and air conditioning, sanitation, labor saving appliances, furniture, clothing – at greatly reduced costs.

10. The base of formal education and further access to knowledge has been greatly expanded. An exceptional number of young people are now able to go to college.

11. The openness of society has been increasing. The roles of women and minorities have become more equal, more permissive and more productive.

12. As a result of these changes, real incomes have doubled between 1900 and today. In 1900, the "middle class" was just about 1% of the population. Now it is over 23%. Poverty as a human affliction is remarkably down all over the world. In a study of 10 countries,

eight showed a reduction of people living in poverty from 1.1 billion to just 782 million, and real gains have been experienced to a remarkable degree in China and India, and in unlikely countries such as Bangladesh, Vietnam, Cambodia, Ethiopia and Congo

13. There is a very special reality that, through the 1980s and '90s, the U. S. accepted more than a million legal immigrants per year – more legal immigrants than all other nations of the world combined. In addition, there has been a huge flow of illegal immigrants. 11% of the U. S. population is foreign born – about 40 million people. And it has been ever more clear that the performance of immigrants and refugees has been overwhelmingly positive.

14. Factoring out immigration, the rise of American inequality greatly disappears; for 89% of the American population, that is native born, income inequality has been declining since the 1960's. For African-Americans, family median incomes are finally currently rising twice as fast as the population as a whole.

15. 80% of the U. S. population has graduated from high school, and 25% have a college degree. The U. S. averages 12.3 years of education – the highest in the world. The current drop-out rate is about 10%; but prior to 1940, most children dropped out – because they had to go to work.

16. In 1900, 42% of workers were in primary sectors of the economy; 38% were in industry; and 20% were in "white collar" occupations. 47% of women's employment was as domestics. 58% of men and 52% of women are now in service sector. In 1850, the average work week was 66 hours; in 1900, it was 53 hours; in 2000, it was 42 hours. House keeping chores took 4 hours a day for 90% of housholds in 1900; in 2000, it is about 14%.

In sum, despite the negativism and hand-wringing, and the problems that still need to be solved, Americans have developed a great and rewarding country. The people themselves have favored moderation, have exhibited a fund of common sense, and have displayed the kind of courage their leaders have often lacked.

GOVERNANCE AS THE ART OF BEING HUMAN

What we deal with in the world of American politics is simply the implacable conflicts inherent in human kind. The world is never risk free; there cannot be created a risk-free world. What can be done is for the people themselves, despite the eternal conflict between conformity and dissent, to demand that their leaders be more positive and supportive, and do not exacerbate these conflicts for shoddy political advantage. We must somehow stop the government's preoccupation with "can't", or with "us vs. them". Human choice is the natural opponent of control and regulation. The Moderate Party should see itself not as the party of centrist power or of Blockade or Stalemate, but as the party of intergovernmental collaboration. Collaboration is a whole different concept. It means that governments can and should deliberately combine to produce results even where each may have its own policy imperatives. In other words, government plans and programs must not be forced into conflict, and can instead be manipulated into collaboration and shifted to laws, policies and regulations that are simpler, shorter and based more on principles of guidance and away from the urge to create restrictions and prohibitions. If this were to happen, it would produce a desirable reduction of challenges and law suits over the enforcement of government's vast layer of control. People yearn to believe that "the rule of law" will define all that is good and proper, but the rule of law is not enough, since the laws themselves can be perverted or ignored. What people really want in life is security, stability and fairness. What this demands of governments is moderation, common sense and courage.

All governance has escalated in power and complexity. In many world countries government authority is not shared but centrally dictated and controlled. In the United States, the basic government philosophy has always been the use of multiple levels of government, each with its own defined roles and scope and degrees of influence. What has emerged then is a great and compelling range of vital public programs that are shared in, and led by many complex relationships between governments. Consider the following list of reasons why government sharing and collaboration are vital:

1. Sharing power promotes democracy because it is easier for citizens and organizations to reach and influence local governments. Especially with social services programs, most national governments are seen as remote and preoccupied with broader issues. Decentralization also enhances the total number and competence of public leadership.

2. Local governments offer the potential of achieving higher public service effectiveness and responsiveness, and of creating a better and more capable public service. In general, local administration of public programs is seen as more practical and less theoretical or doctrinaire. Program success is more likely to be evaluated in terms of how well the public is served.

3. Devolution will take power out of the hands of centrist elites, reduce elitist collusion and the power of centrist government organizations, and reduce the range of public activities that are vulnerable to corrupt control. It also importantly shifts the attention of special interest lobbying groups from a single target to a variety of governments, more attuned to the general public interest.

4. As more power and authority is decentralized, it makes the relationship between the central government and local governments more balanced since these relationships will be more often negotiated rather than dictated. Regional governments have roles to play which are genuinely regional in nature – for example, regional road nets, the allocation of land uses, the provision of public utilities or the priorities between conflicting demands on government. But to achieve these advances, regional and municipal governments must be independent and not just administrative units of the central government.

Political Doctrine

Every government is a political state, and each has constructed a doctrinal framework articulating some broad and generalized form of governance. The most prominent political frameworks in use today are communism, state socialism, representative democracy and centrist authoritarianism. None of these frameworks are absolute, and they often overlap or are in conflict in some very confusing ways. But in each country the prevailing political framework is seen as a vital way to explain and justify the policies of the government to the people, and to provide a test of acceptability for each encountered public policy issue. Different versions of the predominant political doctrine may be constantly in conflict, but this is normally seen as healthy. Socialism vs. capitalism; the "right" vs. the "left"; Republicans vs. Democrats—all bring vigor and change and keep the political doctrine from being too rigid. It is simply not possible for any government to invent a new political theory for every new issue. Therefore, political parties or interests are constantly negotiating the practical consequences of political doctrine, and the results are used to define what is right and wrong.

The United Nations has repeatedly sought to define a world-wide array of international development goals, which are in fact a compelling moral statement of what should be the ideal set of political doctrines. The Millennium Development Goals as defined anew in 2016 are as follows:

1. Eradicate extreme poverty and hunger
2. Achieve universal primary education
3. Promote gender equality and empower women
4. Reduce child mortality
5. Improve maternal health
6. Combat HIV/AIDS, malaria and other diseases
7. Ensure environmental sustainability
8. Develop a global partnership for development.

Obviously, it would be hard for anybody to object to any of these noble objectives, but they should be seen primarily as a somewhat pompous assertion of all that is seen as good and noble. Compliance by nations is voluntary and the UN itself cannot make compliance happen. And it is certain that any degree of success will be claimed by the UN as the result of their goal setting. Meanwhile, other agonizingly serious problems have not been recognized. For example, 161 of the 196 countries of the world have enthusiastically endorsed the UN Convention Against Corruption, including almost all of the enthusiastically corrupt regimes in the world. Countries where starvation is desperate, or children are malnourished, or women are treated unequally are all dutiful signatories of the Millennium Goals.

Cultural Imperatives as Doctrine

Every society is really based on its culture, which is a combination of ethnic, religious, racial, tribal and social mores. Social coherence is imbedded in deeply felt concepts of survival and self-protection, identity, mutual support, and broad judgments about what is good and bad, and what needs support or resistance. The more forcefully these cultural mores are held, the more they tend to become doctrine that must be defended and not allowed to change. Cultural values must be honored by the government, whether they seem rational or not. Thus, "good" governments are those that find a way to accept these values and incorporate them into policy.

One of the most powerful of these cultural mores is the sense of nationalism - the importance of national coherence and sense of nationhood beyond tribalism or narrow geographical identity. In a sense, nations are what tribes become—broader, more inclusive, more powerful, and with higher potential. Nations become more future oriented and more instrumental, and "what is good for the country" becomes a powerful determinant of what governments decide to do.

Most people have a strong willingness to be responsible. Flowing through society are two human tides: a preference for stability, status quo, and an inertia against "change"; and then a striking enthusiasm among many for adventure; for bold action; for trying something new – an appetite for challenging uncertainty. This is not either/or. Both are high cultural influences and both are culturally important and necessary.

Moderation may seem radical if it substantially alters the current philosophy. "Socialism" described by current liberal politicians is not really socialism in the sense that it directly controls the economy and allocates the means of production. What people admire is a government that attends to the real needs of people, but this is really human social responsibility, far broader than the control philosophy of state socialism. And in fact, America is really dividing into three main streams, none of which have any real basis in socialism. Increasingly, the country is seeing the emergence of a genuinely black society, and perhaps, soon a genuine Hispanic society. These three societies can either be in conflict, or they can work out forms of compatibility and collaboration. It would be the objective of the Moderate Party to be relevant and constructive in working out such collaborative relationships.

THE MODERATE PARTY AGENDA

1. Make the government and the party advocates of collaboration and cooperation and not contention and opposition.
2. Base the philosophy of the government on a strong commitment of personal responsibility.
3. Make the basic fundamental intent to be the well-being of the people and not the government or political parties.

THE NATURE OF AMERICAN GOVERNMENT

Some form of governance has existed among humans from the dawn of time, beginning with the coherence of families to the bonding of clans, on to a long and complex process by which power in human affairs evolved to become more concentrated and deliberately projected. Clans became tribes, and tribes became nations. The more or less democratic forms of clan chieftains and tribal councils became parliaments and almost inevitably, these systems concentrated power and control in the hands of often dictatorial leaders. Power became the legitimate instrument of the State – the power to decide, to create facilities and services, and to develop sub systems for performance and control. The power included the ability to extract resources from the country and to decide how to deploy them. It remains generally legitimate that government power can create and maintain a military to protect the nation; or to create and maintain a system of police and courts and systems of laws for the domestic safety and security of the nation's citizens. In developing nations where private enterprises were not sufficiently developed, the government has been a legitimate option for the creation or expansion of critical elements of the economy. The government is generally accepted as a force to limit crime or terror or other unacceptable citizen conduct. These roles of government are needed and constructive – until they become excessive and oppressive.

But it is inevitable and immutable that the tides of change are always flowing, and as the world changes and becomes far more complex, different demands are placed on people and their governments. Individual people adapt because they are forced to do so to live with the new realities. Human

7

institutions both public and private have a certain degree of ability to choose their fate, and they have responded to change in a wide variety of ways. But every government ever created, for the last 10,000 years has possessed critical characteristics which seeks to oppose change. Government leadership has almost always been in the hands of a relatively small and highly centrist ruling elite. Such governments are strongly inclined to produce a powerful, often oppressive leader; they stoutly resist change because it might produce a loss of power and control. Thus, they cannot abide opposition or even criticism, however modest. Few people realize that any government can, if it wishes to do so, involve itself in virtually anything and everything in the country. Why and how governments do this is endlessly complex and muddled and conflicting; endlessly arrogant and often dangerous.

In a very real sense, the norm for governments has been authority from the top down, even in the face of a fair degree of social coherence, as for example the enduring strength of tribes, clans, regions and beliefs. But centrism is the father of preferment, which is the father of corruption. What is missing is the sense of the need for the government to be accountable or to be efficient and productive. It is far more difficult to forge a government based on unity, cooperation and mutual support among people. But the absolute essential is for people to be self-sufficient. The inevitable curse of State Socialism is the argument that the collective good of the people overpowers the motivations of individual people. But the imposition of some form of collective will is inherently unfair, because the people themselves are inherently fair. It is argued that "uncontrolled" differences are somehow "wrong" and must be prevented. In truth, it is just people being human, and no system of government ever invented has ever had more validity than that of people being human. It is better to be "fair" than to be "right" by some government standard. It is better to obey the best of human relations than it is to obey the Rule of Law.

The Moderate Party should never depart from the great principle of personal self-sufficiency. Its policies should always support and promote and defend the ability of people to act in their own best interests. It must deliberately design itself as much as possible as a coalition of interests which have as their base and strength being built from the bottom up; from organizations dependent on individuals aligning themselves in groups which are capable of influencing major decisions and actions, often in opposition to more traditional top down political domination. In the United States now this concept is being challenged and made worse by the fact that today's left has moved strongly to a favoring of group identity, based on race, gender, sexual preference, location or civic favoritism.

What are these bottom up elements? They will be local communities of people who can form around thousands of bonds of mutual support and self-interest. They can be formed around race, gender, religion social conviction, neighborhoods or even job sites or kinds of skills. Businesses have strong motives to promote their own interests, often against the authority of government. Local governments should protect the interests of their own citizens first, even while they are also national citizens. People's lives are first and foremost local lives.

An extraordinarily important evolution is happening in the manner is which wealth is distributed. Old concepts of rich vs. poor are now tending toward a universal middle class – of low, of middle, and of upper ranges. The super-rich are resisted in part because increasingly they are seen as having gone beyond a legitimate level of achievement and become immoral, and that they achieved their dominance by improper means involving the implacable application of special interest politics within a tainted political system.

It is therefore extremely important for the Moderate Party to push wherever possible for the disaggregation of power; devolution and delegation to local governments; more delegation to local elements of central governments; the separation of political parties in the control of state mechanisms.

This is not meant to preclude the necessary and substantial involvements by governments in human affairs. It is to avoid the fatal error of substituting the control of the State against the capacity for human self sufficiency. It is a marvelous reality that, in fact, to a degree that is not adequately realized, American policy can and does take care of itself. Yes, the government, yes the public programs, but also yes the strength of society in general. And elements of society have always played a vital third role. There are literally hundreds of thousands of private organizations dedicated to providing help and care and assistance to the poor and disadvantaged. This is humanity at its best. These organizations range from small neighborhood groups to major international organizations. They are most often funded by private donations, and are heavy users of volunteer workers, but many are also agents of governments and receive substantial government financing.

There are universities full of people who are studying the most worthy and noble modern theories of governance, but it is important to study governance on the dark side. One great failure is the far too human gap between pompous intellectual utterance and the enormous difficulty of actually getting anything done. So much of the decision making in governments is emotional and not essentially rational, and many of these motives are destructive – an urge for power, a greedy desire to get very rich, a cult of corrupt alliances, hatred of something or someone. Meanwhile, the general population is largely passive, feeling powerless and intimidated by oppression. The government itself will often create and exacerbate conflicts between elements of society; if people can be taught to hate each other, they may hate government less.

But the world has always found itself trying to deal with a wide variety of human dysfunctions. There is a whole range of <u>eternal</u> conflicts between people in families, clans, tribes, villages, regions, races and religions. There are further equally eternal conflicts between men and women, old vs. young, rural vs. urban, rich and poor, race, religion, and many, many others. Then there are our modern conflicts deliberately created: between political parties; between Communists and democrats; State Socialism vs. individualism; and the totally incomprehensible 1400 year Islamic history of Sunni vs. Shia. In fact, governments – at least good and effective governments – are perhaps the most difficult thing thing that human beings are called upon collectively to do. What people need to understand is that running a government involves not only local politics but also a command of the worlds of economic development, social services, public infrastructure, finance, national culture, environment, foreign relations, and powerful human yearnings for well-being, peace, stability and even "progress". Governance has become a world of incomprehensible complexity and irreconcilable conflict. It is extraordinarily difficult to find people who can deal with such complexity, or to design institutions to assure adequate control.

In relatively well-run countries like the United States, there is a reasonable recognition that the government does really important and necessary things, and does most of them reasonably well. There may be little difference between the levels of performance by public organizations and private ones. But many people feel that their government has gotten out of hand; is running amok and exceeding its reasonable roles, or that it just takes care of itself and not the people. As the nature of governments becomes more authoritarian, the view from the bottom up becomes more fearful, involving feelings of increasing risk, and a growing sense of constriction of freedom of action. There remains the fond hope, mostly expressed by the advocates of representative democracy, that governance will ascend to a level of cooperation, persuasion, mutual respect, and the application of power through common sense and moderation.

But the modern world remains full of bad governments – corrupt, uncaring, incompetent, wasteful, unjust, oppressive and dictatorial. Bad governments always produce counter reactions from citizens. Those counter reactions may range from legitimate political opposition or to vigorous resistance to the government's policies and actions, all the way to armed conflict, insurrection and even civil war. Public resistance to bad governments may be seen as justified and deserving of success at some level, but there is much simple human inertia, and stubborn resistance to "change". The issue becomes when such opposition can reach some fundamental characteristics of rightless and reality. Many in the U. S. believe they see portents of increasing "badness".

The main motives of national oppressors seem to blend the urge for power, advancement of some cause, and/or serious greed; but also hopefully in most countries some sense of responsibility to advance the welfare of the country and its people. But tyrannies are all too often successful, and oppressive regimes are remarkably complex and resistant to pressure and change. Tyrants are often motivated by strange combinations of perverse psychology, questionable rationalizations, and flawed visions of reality. In many cases, the success of an insurgency produces a "I am the liberator" leader who then uses that justification to perpetuate outrages against the people who have supposedly been "liberated". In other words, the old tyrants are often simply replaced by new tyrants.

There are other forms of perverse psychology: a high capacity to ignore reality, the grip of some powerful prejudice, the dominant desire to control. Once in power, there is an almost overwhelming attitude to anchor power so that it is beyond challenge. And of course, in the worst-case situations, dozens of governments have pushed far beyond "unfair" to the point of being actively oppressive and dangerous. Many top down governments have indeed become tyrannical, abusive, murderous and deadly, so that even average citizens are in constant fear for their own lives, their families, their property, their well-being, and their freedom.

Finally, there is the fearful admission of the existence of genuine evil. It is simply true that some situations can be explained only by recognizing that a tyrant is absolutely evil and is driven by the urge to inflict pain and to do irreparable harm. This is not artificial tactics; it is basically inexplicable horror.

The American government has managed mostly to avoid these malfunctions. It now finds itself dealing with four great tides, each of which creates a set of demands that must be satisfied and then must be financed:

1. The provision of basic elements of government; a directing organization of government leadership and management of crucial activities; the provision of public services; a legal/judicial/court/police system; a military establishment for defense of the country; and a national system for currency and banking.
2. The demands of special interests vs. the general public interest.
3. The tides of population increase, national growth, the reality of change, the shift of populations to cities, and the heightening of societal sophistication.
4. Mounting national divisiveness and political and social stalemate.

The tide, especially since WWII, has been for governance to assume a broader and deeper role in American society. Not only are there more people, but their perception of the responsibilities of government has changed. Thus, not only are there more children, but it is now universally assumed that they have a **right** to education at least through secondary grades, and increasingly, the sense that a university education should also become a right, and possibly free like primary education. It is no longer enough to have adequate sources of health care available. It is now believed that health care must be provided for all people, even if that means that more of the cost must be borne by governments. Two lane roads become eight lane highways. Hundreds of airports have sprung up. Millions of acres have become national lands and their care and maintenance publicly financed. The elderly must be cared for, often at public expense. The unemployed must be publicly supported – and on and on.

The modern American economy has slowly evolved into a far more complex and often disturbing set of relationships between the government and private business. Public money is provided to private organizations in hundreds of strange and mysterious ways through the tax system, the public budget, and the structure of regulations.

In sum, as governance has become broader and more sophisticated, it has inevitably become far more expensive. It is very important to understand this reality: the potential system at all levels will be fed and lubricated by its ability to spend. It is wonderfully rewarding politically to be the provider of some public good or service. It seems infinitely painful for politicians to say no. As a consequence, government has simply burgeoned. It is an engine that can move in only one direction. There is little effective constraint and little ability to refuse or reform. Nor is this expansion a response to any coherent plan or sense of defined purpose or sense of limitation.

All of this must be funded. Each of the hundreds and hundreds of public programs must be financed. The Catalog of Federal Domestic Assistance now lists more than 1000 federal grant programs. Each of these programs requires a government organization and staffs and delivery mechanisms, creating a whole a second range of costs in addition to the costs of the programs themselves. And the fact that the government operates at a deficit means that there is an additional cost through the financing of enormous government debt itself.

Then there are two additional tides. America is so alluring that it attracts immigrants from all over the world. There are now about 40 million people who immigrated to this country, legally and illegally, during the last 2-3 decades. In the short term, they are costly. It is hoped and expected that in the long term they will be productive. Then, since WWII, America has been the most extensive participant in international relationships, and there again, there are major demands for financial support for an urgent and growing range of assistance demands in every part of the world. With the new wave of national conflicts and terrorist oppression, this need can truly become the proverbial bottomless pit.

Thus, the size and range of the government seems destined to continue to expand and to challenge the acceptance of the American public. Increasingly, many people are willing and able to construct a counter power base which can offer some protection from mandated government from the top down, and provide a base for negotiations with a very demanding centrist regime. Local governments are able to argue their own interests versus the centrist control. Private companies are automatically a counter force against government oppression, but on the other hand, private special interest groups can bargain their support of the regime in exchange for protection and preferment. The military, the police, and lately the intelligence services always form their own power centers. Corruption can be used to strike deals between the crooked parties.

The bottom up world has two further levels of functioning. In the first, there will be people who oppose a regime, but do not try to overthrow it. Instead, they insert themselves into elements of the establishment, hoping to mitigate its excesses, and to push forward moderating positions and ideas.

This is the essence of the current stance of the two American political parties. This is an extraordinarily long-term approach, but it is often the one that works. Governments do moderate themselves. Other people simply decide that the safe course is just to "go along to get along", hoping to dodge any stray bullets on the way. But many people are willing and able to construct a counter power base which can offer some protection and provide a base for negotiations with the holders of power.

Some of the patterns of governance are so horrible that they surpass rational understanding. The more one studies the roles of bad governments, the more one is forced to accept the fact of human evil. After all of the excuses are examined and rejected, and motivations are explained, and not believed, there remains a horrible number of human actions that are inhuman and insane, and utterly beyond rational explanation. The United States constitutional system, and the positive attitudes of the great majority of the population have succeeded in protecting the country against such horrors.

Governments are always "top down"; people are "bottom up". Governments are necessarily about the exercise of power. National leaders are almost by definition centrists in character, and most of the philosophies that have been developed about how to run a government are highly centrist as well, ranging from the pharaohs as gods, to the divine right of kings, to Communism, State Socialism or the Islamic Caliphate. Even representative democracy, in modern times, has a strong tendency to justify the supposed need for more and more direction from the top. The ultimate level of bottom up activity is armed resistance to the regime: street protests, anti-government actions, attacks on government officials and facilities, insurrections, or civil war. These forms of action are excruciatingly difficult and dangerous. In some cases, regimes of crooks and scoundrels are overthrown, only to be replaced by a new group of crooks and scoundrels. But the glory is that many such drastic bottom up surges have triumphed.

Beyond the governments that are merely bad are the governments that descend to the level of human evil. After all of the excuses are examined and rejected, and motivations explained and not believed, there remains a horrible number of human actions that are inhuman and insane, and utterly beyond rational explanation. Many of these actions are perpetrated by individuals or small groups, but these actions can inflict unbelievable death and destruction. Terror groups like Boko Haram in Nigeria, or al-Qaeda or ISIS may posture that they are saving people from corrupt and inept governments, but they cannot conceivably offer any explanation that justifies the nature of the hellish attacks against defenseless people and the deliberate slaughter of innocents, including even the smallest of children. Americans need to understand how fortunate they are because our governance and society have largely been able to avoid sinking into these bottomless pits.

II. Public Policy

There is an urgent need to develop more adequate ways to face up to the most basic policy question of all: what are the legitimate and necessary purposes of governments? Are there not areas of national activity that are not cast as obligations of government control? The realistic answer is yes, and it would be possible to develop a new public policy attitude to seek out and do away with such activities.

The philosophical conflict discussed above is fully articulated in debates over the public policies that drive government. One conflict is that centering around the government vs. the private sector. One extreme is the socialist philosophy to constrain the private sector and deploy a form of government control instead, but this extreme has been rejected in the U. S. At the next level is the real U. S. model with the private sector dominant in economic terms, but with the government locked in a vastly complex and sophisticated set of interrelationships with it, both good and bad. The other extreme would be a society and economy with minimum governmental primacy, but this has long been abandoned in the U. S. Governments in the United States have played out literally hundreds of these debates, almost to the point where, in major arenas of national activity, it is extraordinarily difficult to tell where the private sector ends and the government begins.

This is the same dilemma facing governments in the arenas of social services and public infrastructure. It is really very human to ask for "more". It is sort of natural for politicians to want to say "yes", but they are pressed by conflicting motives: a desire to be positive and helpful; a somewhat cynical urge to say "yes" as a populist measure to promote political backing; and the need as a public official to be efficient and prudent in the disbursement of public money.

The interpretation now is growing: the demands for "more" have not been adequately resisted. Special interest politics are now excessive and ominous. The political system has failed adequately to protect the public purse. Without allowing this argument to be addressed simply along political party lines, it is increasingly necessary for all of the political leadership to find the courage to be more constraining and judgmental against any excessive and unwarranted demands against the sources of public money. A more stringent acid test is needed: to resist funding programs in which there is no legitimate federal interest or responsibility, and/or which are clearly designed to favor some special interest and not the general public. A policy must be defined that seeks to reduce, rather than increase, demands on the public budget. Each line item in every government budget should be subjected to assessment as to whether it can be pared down or eliminated, or have its marginal beneficiaries removed. There can be great value in concentrating available funds on those with greatest needs.

It is possible that what has emerged over time is a government so complex that it cannot be governed, and such complexity is the enemy of democratic understanding. There is no such thing as "the government". What exists is a great, huge, extraordinarily complex, complicated and utterly incomprehensible mass of organizations and relationships. And experience has proved that what the people really want is often very different than what politicians think is good for them. Is it even possible to simplify this vast complexity? Probably not much, within the limits of today's weak political courage. But it is important therefore to argue that government laws should be kept as simple as possible, and within the range of what people can understand if they try. A target should be to define the "least" government that is consistent with national need and intent. As collateral to this reasoning, the more complex and confusing a body of laws become, the more possibilities are created for misuse and corruption. Therefore, laws should be written to meet the general public good and this standard should always be held up against legislation proposed merely for the advantage of some special elite or specific special interest. It is astonishing to learn that a number of public programs are operating under enabling statutes which have expired, but nobody seems to have the guts to call for their termination.

The Constitution and supporting legislation should clearly authorize the conduct of political parties, and preferably they should y down the rules for honest elections in some detail if possible. Constitutional definition of proper elections would highlight the nature of such pathology and provide a stronger basis for opposition to a system that is increasingly not only smelly but ineffective.

Also, if possible, Constitutions or basic laws should provide mechanisms to prevent the abuse of presidential appointment powers, or the "reinterpretation" of laws. Since time immemorial, perhaps the greatest problem of governments has been the overwhelming application of executive power. Sometimes, such power is just seized, and is beyond control, but where there is some formal framework for the definition of power, its limits should be established and carefully asserted.

Politicians have always known the popular appeal of providing public goods and services, and many have cynically used this fact to curry the support of people as voters. The intent of this approach is deliberately perverse. It spends public funds not necessarily to deal with legitimate public needs, but simply to direct funds to the things that would produce votes. This misdirection of public expenditure may have serious consequences in those areas that are neglected. A classic example is the case where the government wants to provide very cheap bread for urban dwellers, and in order to do so, the government will distort the pricing structure from beginning to end. It will deliberately set prices paid to the farmers who grow the grain – often so low that they make no profit, or even get forced into a loss. Then, millers of the grain are underpaid; the bakers of bread are underpaid; but bread is cheap, and the urban population happily votes for their government benefactors. Populism in this political sense is a deliberate policy choice and can be applied across an extraordinary range of activities - gas and fuel oil, food, clothing, housing, electricity and water, communications, and of course who gets to pay taxes. But it seems clear that U. S. wellbeing would be advanced if this perversity is stoutly resisted.

Politics vs. management is a conflict almost entirely played out inside governments, and almost always, bad politics makes bad management. The American public is largely unaware of one of the great hidden policy conflicts that is taking place in the hundreds of government programs and projects. Each program is created and financed by basic enabling statutes, and the formal political leadership has a quite proper right and obligation to oversee the proper conduct of these programs and the validity of funding deployment. And yet, each year, there are <u>hundreds</u> of situations where perverse political decisions overpower common sense and managerial decision making. The political system has created governments that suffer from programs and projects that, by any rational evaluation, are unnecessary, ineffective, low payoff, duplicative, obsolete or of low value. Some of these political demands are simply illegal, such as those that represent bribes, deliberate overpayments, improper contracting or nepotism and political preferment. In most cases, political distortions are not illegal but they are certainly inappropriate, blatantly irrational or arrogantly outrageous.

The classic game that is perhaps most recognized by the American public is the game played by members in legislative bodies from top to bottom, called "the earmark" or the "set aside". Congressional members are constantly on the hunt to identify ways to seek money for their legislative district out of some government agency. It does not matter whether the cost is justified; for them, the only criterion for justification is "give it here – or else!" For example, the Pentagon has long maintained a sophisticated information system which shows how much money flows to every Congressional district in the country, and there is a deliberate policy to make sure that somehow every district gets something out of the money pump. The public should understand that many of the political earmarks are payoffs run against the realities of managerial evaluations, or even of common sense, real need, or cost effectiveness as bad politics makes bad management time and time again. There have been two or three efforts in Congress, or by the President or some governor to prohibit or impede the tide of perverse earmarks. Some have succeeded for a while, but all seem eventually to fade, and this hidden policy seems to be immortal. What is the ultimate solution to the dilemma of weak incompetent politics? It is for the American voting public to stop electing cowards, fools and incompetents.

The U. S. government wisely and thankfully avoided the great surge of State Socialism that swept through the rest of the world after WWII. We can congratulate ourselves now, as Socialist governments all over the map have been forced by economic and social failures and incompetence to move reluctantly back to a broader private sector, and more bottom-up democracy. In the end, State Owned Enterprises (SOEs) proved not to be so much efficient instruments of economic development, but highly inefficient economic vehicles, most of them running at congenital deficits, to the great embarrassment of the socialist politicians that were forced to defend them.

There are numerous vital lessons that the U. S. can learn from the Socialist experience. All too often, economic operations proved to be heavily impacted by ceaseless elements of political intervention into their supposedly superior economic capability, and thus, SOEs are now being disposed of in many countries, and this tide should be continued. Capital for creation and development of SOEs has been provided by governments at little or no cost, while private companies have generated such funds themselves or borrowed for the purpose. But still, in the end, the total cost within the national economy is far better through private asset creation than for heavy taxes to finance incompetent SOEs.

The lesson to be learned in the U. S. out of this almost universal negative experience is not only that state enterprises are dangerous, but more importantly that it is at the very great advantage of our government to become committed to the support and stimulation of private enterprise. This however has been a constant dilemma in the U. S. for almost 200 years. Tax, yes; but not "too much". Regulate, yes; but not beyond reason. Encourage, yes; but not subsidy and preferment.

But the U. S. has still had to struggle with advocacy groups who espouse some of the more important elements of State Socialist policy. For example, during the 2017 presidential election campaign, Senator Bernie Sanders declared himself to be a "democratic Socialist", and he enthusiastically advocated such popular socialist policies as free public college education, universal government funded health care, and fuller "tax the rich" policies. Remarkably, President Trump has toyed with the imposition of new taxes on foreign imports into the U. S., apparently unaware that this is an old socialist policy, known widely in socialist governments as ISI: "Import Substitution Initiatives". This policy theory was that taxing potential imports would prevent their entry, thus protecting domestic producers and service providers. The almost universal reality was that ISI left the natives with domestic goods that were more expensive and of lower quality, and local businesses were prevented from getting vital imports that they needed to develop.

A very similar policy argument centers around people. Some policy advocates seek to prevent the entry of foreign immigrants and refugees because they are seen as "taking jobs away" from domestic workers. Closed borders were a hallmark of great Socialist regimes such as the USSR and China. But here, the consequence seems the same. Many immigrants in fact possess widely needed and wanted skills and abilities, and their record over several decades of U. S. experience has that they have made valuable contributions to national wellbeing. In other cases, low skilled workers are still eagerly sought for certain kinds of jobs such as crop collection where the domestic workforce is not large enough. In sum, under an open borders policy, the U. S. has allowed immigration of more than 40 million people both legal and illegal – far more than any other country in the world.

In essence, policies seeming to stem from the Socialist base are justified in the U. S. as being more humanist than "greedy capitalism", and that democratic socialism would be offered by a noble and caring government. The counter policy position is that, in reality, socialist governance in almost all of its manifestations represented more control and domination than it did assistance and service. Almost all socialist governments have been economic disasters and serious cultural disappointments.

One of the first and most enduring forms of government national involvement has been a remarkable set of government interventions into rural and small-town life. Over several decades, government policies have been based on the premise that rural America is under-developed both economically and socially, and that it was necessary to maintain a comprehensive set of government policies and programs to bring rural/small town areas forward. At the same time, reality has been that the American future is already urban, that cities and suburbs are burgeoning, that 81% of the population is now in cities. Rural America meanwhile is well able to take care of itself. It might be reasonably argued that current rural wellbeing is largely the result of all of those decade-long government support programs. In any event, it is time to face up fully to the new opportunity: deliberately and drastically cut back on no longer needed government largess, and reinvest the money in programs for the urban poor.

It is widely recognized that a very large generation of citizens is now moving inevitably into the age of retirement, and this surge is demanding some "retooling" of public policies. Is the health care system sturdy enough to support the needs of this aging population? Will the economy stand up to a great decline in the numbers and the earning power of these retirees? Are retirees financially able to support themselves in retirement? If there are large numbers of people who are physically or financially unable to care for themselves, who will care for them – their sons and daughters or the government? If the burden assumed by the government is greatly more expensive, where will the money come from?

Much of the answer to these questions is already apparent. People may be able to draw upon the Social Security retirement system, and they will become eligible for Medicare or perhaps Medicaid. Their taxes will be radically reduced. There are special programs for the elderly who suffer from many forms of disability. Most will probably be covered by some form of retirement earned by work in a company. Many will be covered by retirement programs provided for civil service retirement programs or those provided by the military.

In fact, studies show a reassuring pattern: of people over the age of 65, more than 80% say that there are financially "safe", and at least 80% say that their financial resources make them "secure". This creates the prospect for a new and more rational debate about retirement policy; it is possible to more broadly apply a "means" determination to retirement qualification, where the relatively well-off receive less, and the money flows instead to the most needy. It might also make sense to recognize the increasing physical well-being of the middle aged, and simply raise the age of eligibility for most social services designed to serve the elderly. Could the lobbyists that constantly demand "more" be induced to argue for "more rational"?

Another possibility, as an option to the battles over "most needy" or "means testing" is for the government simply to force a limitation on any changes to the funding made available for social programs to the rate of inflation, then dispersed to the states as a fixed amount block grant, thus making the states decide on how these limited funds are deployed.

Beginning with the Constitution and continuing through almost 250 years of thousands of laws, regulations, policies, programs, actions, interpretations and pleas, the United States has sought to maintain a policy where people may be separate and distinct in their lives and culture while remaining equal under the law. Here surely is a policy that has never fully succeeded. Women, minorities, the social variant, and the economically disadvantaged all feel that their world remains unequal and often unfair.

As argued elsewhere here, the African American community in America appears to be saying that "equal" does not have to mean "same". Blacks have evolved their own society in all of its manifestations that is separate and equal in legal stature, but parallel to the long traditional culture of white European origin. Is this a good thing for the country? Almost certainly, the answer is yes. And so it may be necessary to start rethinking all kinds of public policy in terms of whether they not only permit, but perhaps enhance the best elements of this equal/parallel world. And it is possible that American society will become even more complex, with a parallel Hispanic culture, and perhaps - an American Muslim culture?

One of the most interesting and potentially powerful tools for government leadership is that of the skills of priority-setting. The current political policy culture is that all demands on the public purse and the public policy base are equal, and that all should be "honored". This is a critical base for the success of special interest politics. If the government says yes to one client demand, it must then say yes to all similar demands. If the government provides subsidies for tobacco, or cotton, or corn, or cows, it must then – as a necessity of populist politics – say yes to subsidies for wheat or hogs or apples or asparagus.

What if the government was able to shift this policy into one calling for priority setting? Priority setting would mean a more useful and powerful assessment of public programs based on <u>value or payoff or outcome.</u> Whatever money is available, it would thus be spent on the top priority activities as defined by need and actual results. As Lord Acton, the illustrious British scientist put it "Gentlemen: we have run out of money – so it is time to start thinking."

Priority setting does not necessarily mean the total elimination of some low value programs, but may include changes at the margin to buttress high payoff patterns and cut useless or low value program elements. One of the limitations being discussed centers around the proposal that the government's role in social services should be defined by the concept of "the truly needy". Those that are truly needy in either humanitarian or financial terms should be helped by the government, but government programs would not extend to those who can care for themselves, including institutions such as health clinics and universities. One of the main targets for such a limitation would be federal payments for local "community development" – a money pit of limitless depth.

It is expected, and vitally important, that the American government maintain an effective election system at all levels of government, and that such a system be as invulnerable as possible from the perverse expectation that money can buy elections. There is a growing concern that the current election system is far less independent than it used to be. We are now seeing elections in which literally billions of dollars are being spent to control outcomes – even to the extent that there is the fear that money from foreign sources can enter the system and influence the results. It is frankly widely known that political contributions, made by special interest organizations have a decisive influence on elections and on the minds of those whom the funds support. And once such a candidate is elected, he/she feels compelled to favor their funding backers with decisions impacting their reach into the largess of public programs. It would seem to follow that if sound elections are held, the right people will get elected, and they will do the right things in office. Unfortunately, this is not inevitable. There is a growing perception that those in office are far too passive, and the political system is failing to produce results. Problems that are clearly understood and opposed are simply not dealt with. The system has become ominously inhibited by a preoccupation with divisiveness and sterile infighting between key political leaders. People plead for action, but they get stalemate. They plead for action, but they get passiveness. What is needed is the courage to tackle problems, but instead what is seen is timidity and cowardice. Our political system is built around the need for bottom up cooperation and negotiation, but what we are seeing is opposition and enmity and the triumph of useless and pompous rhetoric.

Immigration into the United States has had a long and valued and honored 200 year history. In the modern era, the U. S. has allowed more than 42 million persons – 31 million legal and 11 million illegal –into our country. We, along with Canada, are by far the most welcoming home for immigrants in the world, and the most sought after. Legal immigrants are required to possess some capacity to sustain themselves. Current laws require that they have some degree of education, some form of skill, a job, or some other support here in the country. They are asked to profess a desire to obey our laws and to seek citizenship if they wish to stay. Illegal immigrants are in a more precarious situation, but even for them, there are paths to ultimate legal residence. Immigration here has never ceased. In fact, threats in other countries are driving more and more people to seek refuge in the U. S. along with the more than one million legal immigrants who enter each year.

The special case of "refugees" is what has seriously muddied U. S. policies. Refuges are those people who claim that they are in great peril in their home countries, and that they fear for their lives and/or the loss of their wellbeing. U. S. laws permit the entry of refugees, but require some validation of the legitimacy of the threats. There are many vastly overburdened courts trying to undertake these proofs. But this is a classic example of the difference between law and justice. To deny entry to a person through the proper application of the law might nevertheless send persons back to a corrupt and oppressive government where they will be killed or brutalized. Sanctuary cities in the U. S. are part of this policy dilemma because these cities argue that their policy may be illegal but it is just and humane.

There are two other critical dimensions to this argument. One is cost. Refugees or illegals gain access to public services and financial aid, to medical care, to assisted housing, and to the education of their children, and somebody has to pay for these things. Is it "fair" to make American citizens pay higher taxes to meet these outsider demands? Isn't this money that might have been spent on our existing urban needy? The ultimate dimension of this debate is the horrible fact that more than 60 million people are refugees somewhere in the world, and it is threatening to think of what it might cost if too many of these unfortunates attempt to throw themselves as a burden onto the U. S. economy and society.

The second issue has to do with the reality that some immigrants and refugees are bad people, or even terrorists infiltrating under the cover of the flow of immigrants and refugees. Some are thieves and crooks. Some are members of vicious gangs like MS-13 who terrorize our urban neighborhoods. Some may be agents of terrorist organizations such as ISIS or al Qaeda who want to attack U. S. interests. This fear is what caused President Trump to deny access to people from certain countries widely seen as sponsoring or harboring such terrorist organizations. Unfortunately, this fear tends to poison relationships at a broader level. There are, for example, people who now hate or fear all Muslims despite the obvious fact that 99% of Muslims are perfectly fine and decent people who suffer most from the viciousness of their own 1%.

One of the crucial elements that emerged in the formulation of the country was the creation of a government structure where individual states would exist formally and legally separate from an overarching federal government. States were intended to stand by themselves with their own laws, revenues and separate policies. Over time however, the laws of separation have not changed but the nature of intergovernmental relations have – in remarkable and utterly confusing ways. There is now almost no facet of American life and culture that is not imbedded in some complex ways with these relationships, and it is now estimated that more than one third of state revenues flow from some federal source. The most compelling of these relationships are those that center around social programs: Medicaid, Social Security, Medicare, unemployment compensation, food stamps, housing and education. But there are hundreds of other programs where the three levels of government are welded together –roads, and bridges, and urban transit and rural development and labor relations and the environment, and citizen equality – and on and on.

Increasing the range and complexity of these relationships has been vigorously pursued in both directions. National policies are often mandated to be carried out at the state level, or by state subsidiaries like counties and cities. State governments benefit from these relationships; but they do not appreciate the Washington tendency toward top down meddling and control. The worst case has become known as the "unfunded mandate" problem where the federal government delegates performance by states but declines to provide the money to carry them out. On the other hand, states and especially cities are masters of easing into Washington to solicit federal funding or to invoke federal leverage in mandating some preferred policy position. It is simply true that many of these demands are a reflection that local politicians have often lacked the courage to generate the tax base to finance their own programs, and they turn to the feds to get bailed out. The author personally experienced this in the federal mass transit program where cities and counties caused the creation of a program of support for local urban transportation that really could not be justified as a true federal responsibility. In addition, the transit agency had to design and enforce a policy called "maintenance of effort" which sought to prevent efforts by local governments to use federal funds to reduce their own funding so that no real total money increase occurred.

So reality is that public policy has, for decades, been aimed at the expansion and intensification of these policy and financial relationships. Is this a good thing or a bad thing? As usual, they will be seen as good of they are pursued with common sense, moderation and courage. They are bad if they are stupid, excessive, of low value and as mere exercises of special interest politics. Let local governments finance their own local services and activities including public transit, law enforcement, schools and facilities construction and management.

What are the best arguments for devolution or decentralization?

a. It promotes democracy because it is easier for citizens to reach and influence local governments, and strengthens the capacities of local governments.

b. Local governments in turn achieve the potential of achieving higher public service effectiveness and responsiveness. In general, local administration of public programs is seen as gaining the ability to be practical, simpler, less theoretical and less constrained by doctrine.

c. It is also argued that, to take some power out of the hands of centrist governments is a good thing. It reduces overburdening control, reduces structural complexity, limits some opportunities for corruption, and diffuses some degree of special interest centrist influence.

d. It is also argued that devolution leads to more balanced negotiations between levels of government. Local governments have many vital roles such as road nets, land use control, public utilities, urban services, etc. Regional governments must be independent and not just administrative subsidiaries of the central government.

e. It is argued that a wiser allocation of scarce government resources is also an economic advantage and that local governments will be smarter about how to improve the value and performance of local economies.

f. These lines of reasoning extend to the complex relationships between state governments and their subordinate country and city jurisdictions.

THE MODERATE PARTY AGENDA

1. The Moderate Party must make as its primary objective not the well-being of the Party but the well-being of the American people.
2. It can and should be a party of collaboration, cooperation and facilitation, and not of opposition, prevention and resistance.
3. It should always prefer the ability of Americans to be self-sufficient and self-supporting and not to become the wards of the government.
4. The self-sufficiency of local governments at all levels should be encouraged.
5. The Party should accept the challenge of finally being a government that GETS THINGS DONE, instead of endlessly talking about it.
6. The Moderate Party must establish and maintain firm opposition to special interest politics when it opposes the best interests of the general public.
7. It must be willing to be a government that limits its roles to those that are "truly necessary" – its's real and crucial roles. It must learn how to say "No".
8. There is a real and compelling responsibility to effectively link the roles of governments to the roles and functioning of the private sector.
9. The Party must recognize that our extraordinarily complex government and society is a drain on the country, and it must commit itself to keep laws and regulation as simple and understandable as possible.
10. No money for votes.
11. Continue to avoid state owned enterprises and reject failed state socialist policies.
12. Continue our fine national record of accepting and integrating immigrants and refugees.
13. Recognize the strength of modern rural and small town life, and cut back needless public subsidy.
14. Support the emergence of the new breadth and depth of black American society, and Hispanic society, and the blossoming of the roles of women.

THE THREAT OF SPECIAL INTEREST POLITICS

One of the most important tides running in governments today is that of the universal presence and power of special interest politics. For a long period, we thought that any expressions of public interest were "good" because they were presumed to be a form of democratic freedom of expression, and they help safeguard the public against a wrong-headed government. But special interest politics have become far more sophisticated and, in most countries including the U. S., far more ominous, and nobody particularly knows what to do about it since most political systems are ideally adapted to it.

It is necessary to distinguish between special interests and "special interest politics". In essence, everybody is involved in special interests in their families, their communities, and their work places. It is therefore natural and normal for people to think and act around their special interests.

At the same time, since politics is so vastly extended and interventionist, a growing proportion of the population now feels threatened by our governments. Yet they want help in protecting their critical interests in the government arena, and in advancing causes in which they believe. People are remarkably willing to invest time, effort, and stress because they think these interests are important. People's reactions can become increasingly both assertive and defensive. They are assertive in pressing for the success of their cause or group, but defensive if they feel that their cause is being threatened or ignored. Neither of these attitudes is likely to be wholly rational; much will be emotional or uninformed. The "special interest" mentality is single minded rather than balanced and refuses to deal with government problems in their whole impact.

Special interests tend to organize themselves so that they have collective influence and a more powerful voice. They will therefore tend to become more formal and bureaucratized, and much more assertive. Offices are opened, professional staffs are hired, funds marshaled, a political agenda decided upon, and lobbying begun to search for allies or resist opponents. This leverage can initially be in the nature of information, education or persuasion, but as these groups press harder, they tend to phase over into "special interest politics" where they actively seek to change laws and regulations to favor their interests, or to capture funds and preferment to aid their cause.

From the political point of view, politicians respond to special interest politics as a powerful means for garnering political support, or at least to avoid active opposition to their political agenda. Once these concessions are gained, they tend to be "forever" and vigorously defended. Subsequent retreat from such concessions is not only regarded as a defeat for the benefited interest group, but probably also as a "betrayal" by their political allies. Governments therefore clash with, and collude with special interest political interests.

Special interest politics are very aggressive and heavily pointed toward the government and what concessions can be obtained – a new program, a subsidy, a tax break, a favorable policy or the overlooking of some wrongdoing. In many cases, there is a professional special interest bureaucracy that exists to lobby the government. These people have to gain something out of the political system from time to time in order to justify their work. And it must be perceived that the "something" that the government grants may be something that it was otherwise not inclined to provide. In other words, the ideal outcome for a special interest bureaucracy is to appear to have wrung concessions or resources from a reluctant government.

A special interest concept has been developed around the idea of "state capture" which has been defined as the actions of individuals, groups or firms both in the public and private sectors to influence and dominate the formation of laws, regulations, decrees, and other government policies to their own advantage. Distinctions can be drawn between the types of institutions subject to capture – the legislature, the executive, the judiciary, or regulatory agencies, or public service delivery organizations like power plants or transport agencies. All forms of state capture are directed toward extracting benefits from the state for a narrow range of individuals, firms or sectors by usurping the basic legal and regulatory framework. They thrive where economic power is highly concentrated, countervailing social interests are weak, and the formal channels of political influence and interest intermediation are underdeveloped.

But the more ominous cases are those in which the influence of special interests is secret and carefully concealed, and deliberately intended as the absolute antithesis of "representative democracy". The history of countries all over the world is filled with this kind of "special interest" politics: the perverse collusion between corrupt officials and countless individuals and groups who are seeking to wrest wealth and power from a fumbling government. What has emerged in every country therefore is a special interest political system based on the following elements:

1. A very broad range of national interests in the hands of the government, with the political system in charge of the decision-making apparatus, and capable of allocating huge resources with some degree of discretion, ranging up to 100% in dictatorships. The more public programs there are, the more special interest groups will be created, and the more intense special interest politics will become, seeking not just money, but power.

2. The system takes place at two levels: first, there will be forms of public debate such as legislative hearings, public utterances, press releases, and endless study commissions. Then there is a second "back room" political process of negotiation and agreement, not visible to the public, which is usually where the real threats and promises are employed. The public operations of government are deliberately designed to be essentially bland assurances, to deflect the public concerns and avoid efforts to penetrate the back-room process.

3. Government's own procedures and program delivery systems which are both massive and ubiquitous and can become vehicles to deliver political preference to special interests. The most important are the public tax system, various forms of government regulations, selectively applied; items in the public budget; the award of government contracts; import and export controls, and of course, simple under-the-table corrupt payments. Both politicians and career civil servants are involved. One of the telltale signs of special interest government is when these delivery mechanisms become so extensive and so technically complex that they defy common understanding, thus giving the people in charge endless opportunities to punish or reward. It is important to recognize this fact: **Special interest politics is enormously successful.**

In Washington, there are now hundreds of offices of registered lobbyists, containing everything from huge staffs in opulent office accommodations down to guys in hallways with cell phones. Even beyond that, there are many organizations and individuals who are trying to leverage the government in some way. The halls of Congress and the corridors of government agencies are indeed crowded with eager throngs of professional pleaders. The nooks and crannies of laws and regulations, budgets, tax codes and administrative procedures quietly show the results of their efforts. It is probably next to impossible to identify and list all of these people and all of their nooks and crannies, but it is one of the major elements of this book to emphasize the overwhelming power that special interest politics has gained over the American political system, so it is important to show the reader a useful listing of the kinds of lobbying influences that govern in Washington.

One specific example shows the nature of such special interest alliances. As reported by Mark Zupan in his book "Inside Job", there has been a special relationship between public unions and state/local government politicians. To quote Zupan, "A critical sector of the U. S. economy increasingly usurped by government insiders is K-12 education which has become more monopolized due to the growing teacher unionization as well as a consolidation of school districts. Such education has become less accountable to the public interest. The growth of union power in public K-12 education mirrors what occurred for state and local government workers in general." He also reflects the serious concern that, in substantive terms, benefits to unions have often been at the expense of educational system effectiveness. Teacher unions have a long, very visible record of political action to promote their own interests. The two leading unions, the American Federation of Unions (AFT) and the National Education Association (NTA) have political influence unrivaled by any other group, and they are among the top donors of funds, mostly to Democratic Party candidates, in presidential, local government and school board elections. They have long been heavily represented in the delegates at political conventions at all levels of government. Teachers have tenure and are very hard to fire, and they are strongly opposed to the idea of more precise teacher performance evaluation, and the whole idea of private charter schools as an option beside government furnished schools.

Imagine that you are Donald Trump – or Barak Obama. What interests could you count on to charge out strongly, either for or against, any policy or program initiative you wish to undertake?

1. Democrats vs. Republicans

2. States, counties, cities, units of local government.
3. Hundreds of race based groups: African Americans, Hispanics, Muslims, Asiatics, and "whites", and a wide range of conflicts within these groups themselves.
4. Dozens of religion-based groups: Christians of many disciplines; Muslims, Jews, Hindus – and the same kind of wide ranging differences within each.
5. Rural/small town interests
6. Literally thousands of industrial and commercial companies in every element and level of the U. S. economy, carrying a wide range of conflicts, attitudes and advocacies.
7. Labor unions, both public and private, which have become among the most important financial contributors to politicians and political campaigns of any element of American society.
8. Hundreds of groups intensely committed to environmental threats, global warming, energy generation and natural resources utilization.
9. Gender groups: mostly women, and in an increasingly sophisticated range of public concerns.
10. The huge "health care" world, with organizations ranging from basic scientific research and down through the whole medical profession and medical plant and equipment to a very high level of interest and concern on the part of millions and millions of people who are both individuals and patients – and also tax payers.
11. The elderly, with a high order of public sympathy and support (after all, eventually, they are us.)

It is usually the ambition of special interest politics to get concessions locked into statute or regulation, since they know that it is infinitely harder to change a law or regulation than to get it enacted in the first place. Thus, these concessions tend to be "forever", with each special interest stoutly defending and protecting them. Special interest groups tend to be implacable, insatiable and immutable – and often insufferable. A listing, in no particular order, of the special interests that generally support the U. S. Democratic Party serves to illustrate the near impossibility of political consensus:

Democratic Party officials and staff

Those who want change

Those who do not want change
Urban interests
Farm families and small communities
The elderly, and the retiree establishment
The African American establishment
The environmentalist establishment
Anti-war, anti-military interests
Socialist and "semi-socialist" liberals
Conservationists
Anti-police elements
Unions
Moderate anti-extremists
Black Lives Matter
Animal rights groups
Teachers and teacher unions and organizations
Anti-Republican groups
Anti-Trump groups
Feminists
Consumer rights groups
University liberal interests
Litigation lawyers
The unemployed
SNAP (food stamp) defenders
Welfare recipients
Medicare defenders
Medicaid defenders
Government employees at all levels
Anti-nuclear groups
Home owner/financer interests
Renewable energy interests
The Civil Rights establishment
Religious groups

These groups and interests are generally seen as beneficiaries of the policies and activities of the Democratic Party and their elected officials, and of course, a similar list could be shown for the Republican Party. For both parties, the demands from these groups, separately and in concert create an almost intolerable pressure.

This kind of list has a crucial importance. It helps people to understand something of this intolerable pressure, and it begs the question of how all of these institutions apply that pressure. All of them live by making demands upon governments, and their general philosophy is the demand for "more": more money, more benefits, more preferment. These interests almost always cloak themselves in the garb of public benefit, and indeed some interests such as women's rights, or African American rights, or support for the poor and elderly have broad public bases and support. But ultimately, most will press their own advantage, not as disinterested supporters but as clients with expectations, rather than advocates of the best interest of the general public.

Why do politicians agree so easily? Special interest politics is not just campaign contribution money or short-term political support. It is more importantly about the forging of longer-term alliances for mutual advantage. The special interest group will continue to provide support as long as the politician continues to deliver. And once a politician is committed publicly to a position, it would be embarrassing to abandon that position, even for just cause, for fear of being perceived as weak or inconsistent, but also for fear that it will outrage special interest backers.

George F. Will, in an article in the Washington Post on November 19, 2017, laments the near fatal impact of a special interest alliance which he characterizes as "the blue model" which he describes as "the iron alliance of the Democratic Party and government workers unions." Under this long term alliance, "unfunded state and local government retirement debt is more than $260 billion and rising. Unfunded pension liabilities for the nation's highest paid government workers are $130 billion and are expected to increase for at least through the next decade. The state is approaching a death spiral: departing people and businesses suppress growth; the legislature responds by raising taxes; the exodus accelerates. The "blue model" is bankrupting cities and states from Connecticut to California."

According to the Federal Election Commission (FEC), of the top 100 contributors to political campaigns, 25 are unions; of the top 25, 13 are unions. The largest contributor in the FEC's data base is the Service Employees International Union, having contributed $ 222 million. The next largest contributor is a private Political Action Committee (PAC) on the west coast called ActBlue which has collected and distributed $149 million, all to Democrats and liberal organizations. The next is another union: The American Federation of State/County/Municipal Employees, contributing $93 million. The National Education Association is next with $92 million, and the American Federation of Teachers is # 6 at $69 million. # 5 is Fahr LLC, another PAC run by Thomas Fahr Stayer, a notable Democrat Party supporter, who has contributed $75 million.

The Democrats love to cite the money contributed to Republican Party causes by the Koch brothers. In fact, the Kochs are 50th on the FEC list at $28 million. But in addition to Act Blue and Fahr cited above, Soros Fund Management is far more generous than the Kochs, having contributed $44 million to the Democratic Party. In general, in contrast to the unions and dedicated supporters who contribute only to the Democratic Party, most corporations contribute to both parties, just in case, but with an edge to the Republicans.

This a classic example of how special interests create powerful and sophisticated linkages among themselves in order to provide mutual leverage. Education and labor groups not only support a liberal government, but will frequently be allies over specific policy issues. Business groups, industry associations, and small business owners will form alliances to support government economic development policies and tax relief issues. Many of these alliances are semi-permanent, but can also be temporary and transient, shifting like a kaleidoscope, depending on the issues under consideration.

In the last analysis, special interest politics, as with all politics, is first and foremost about power and money. While most special interests construct an edifice of public purpose for their position, few make any pretense of seeking for a balance of judgments about the broad public interest, nor are they concerned about the success of the government itself, or the ethics of governance. Special interests can be positive and constructive, but their performance, especially in developing countries, is seriously in doubt.

THE MODERATE PARTY AGENDA

1. It should always be one of the great and enduring principles of the Moderate Party to advance the interests of the general American public over the interests of special interest politics.
2. The Party should become the active advocate of efforts to control the almost uncontrolled spread of special interest politics
3. Of necessity, it is therefore vital to conduct the business of government in as open and transparent a manner possible.

4. Whole more effective means must be developed to design this openness into the formulation of government laws, regulations, administrative procedures and eligibilities for government resources.
5. More intense assessment must be developed to understand and counter the adverse impact of special interest politics on the degree of success of public programs.

WHEN IS GOVERNMENT GOOD? WHEN IS IT BAD?

The quality of American governance requires serious assessment, is a matter of judgment, and is subject to change over time. But there are some general criteria that seem to be so broadly accepted that they can serve as frame of reference and comparison, and as a moral and policy basis for the Moderate Party.

A government, whatever its philosophy or design, can be good when it in fact serves the general public interest – as opposed to serving a series of client special interests, or some narrow elite. Governments should be designed to serve that interest, the policies and processes of public institutions should be dominated by that concept, and public officials should be held accountable to the public interest. History shows that many governments have not lived up to this responsibility, but it is certain that the Moderate Party must start with this basic stance.

A large part of this concept of public service centers on the ability to deal well with the social safety net. This is, or should be, one of the fundamental justifications for government – to provide help to citizens beyond what they can do for themselves, and to protect those in society less able to take care of themselves. This is not state socialism; it is simply the best of human nature.

There are some other things that only governments can do, such as national security, and the provision of key public infrastructure, and there are also things that governments can do better than the private sector, especially in two main areas – the delivery of public services that are outside of the scope of private sector responsibility, and protection of the public from the inadequacies and excesses of the private sector.

Further, governments must protect the public, and assure domestic safety, security and well-being. This means the protection of life and property, and societal peace of mind. But who protects the public from the excesses of government itself? A good government must somehow set limits on its own power, and must be reasonably self-policing and self-reforming. Thus, the Moderate Party.

The public also has a right to demand effectiveness from the government. This should be judged in both political and managerial terms. Politically, the government should be doing the right things; managerially it should be guided by such managerial imperatives as cost-effectiveness, high productivity, rational decision-making (as opposed to failure to decide), timeliness, and honest, respectful service. It has sometimes been argued that democratic governments should not be expected to be efficient — that efficiency is an argument that governments use to excuse the failure to provide adequate public services. But these are two different arguments. The Moderate Party would face up fully to its public responsibilities, provide the services that are needed, and still be effective in management terms.

A highly controversial role is that of governments protecting the public from excesses in the private sector. The socialist political argument, still very much alive, has been that private companies were simply too greedy and would further their own interests even at some harm to the government and to people. Pure private sector advocates counter by saying that the government should stay out of their private affairs, and that government meddling can only hurt the development of private entities. Both of these extreme arguments are fallacious and unrealistic, and bear no resemblance to the modern world. Thus again, the Moderate Party is the answer. It would understand that governments and private sector interests are locked in an enormously complex web of interrelationships. While there are countless sources of conflict between them, the Moderate Party would recognize that these relationships need not be adversarial, and the conflicts are reconcilable. The real objectives are to make these relationships as mutually productive and collaborative as possible, and to maintain a high degree of stability and balance between them. One of the base approaches of the Moderate Party would be positively to create such valuable forms of collaboration.

How then can governments be judged in terms of whether they are good or bad? Over time, several frameworks have been developed that can be used to judge governments. All of them are relevant and in current use. They may seem too philosophical, but in fact, they are given life and vitality by the people who believe in them. They have emerged out of actual human experience and many ways of thinking about human affairs, and they have coalesced into doctrine – a body of principles and motives that are strongly held, and which are used as a guide or framework within which people want to live and make personal decisions, and could be used to shape the policies of the Moderate Party.

- The accretion of power must be controlled, by whatever means are possible. The human attributes of desire for power must be mitigated by elements of governance that keep this urge under control. One of the most dangerous aspects of governance is the reality of personal arrogance. Arrogance is almost always bad, and in governmental terms, it can be dangerous because it involves the use of real power, and arrogant people use this power to oppress. Arrogant leaders tend to believe that they are always "right", and that anybody who opposes them is "wrong". It is wrong and foolish to demand that US government officials should not "talk to" or "deal with" unsavory leaders such as Robert Mugabe, Vladimir Putin of Kim Yong Un. If we followed such a policy, we would have to cut off contacts with half of the governments in the world.

- Another human attribute is greed, and governments typically control huge amounts of wealth. Thus, it must be recognized that greed must be anticipated and limited. It is almost always a threat that greed is activated in the form of corruption, by government officials and the people who want to suborn them. A huge problem is that corruption is very successful and very profitable, and all too seldom prevented. Remember the old saw: "If a public official is honest, he is either a coward or stupid!"

- A common element of political systems is the high energy and zealousness that is generated. Public enthusiasm is highly desirable; excessive zeal may be dangerous. Serious effort must be applied to tell where zeal is too much. A horrible aspect of this concern is that politicians all too often see political advantage in deliberately creating and feeding conflicts between elements of society; rich vs. poor; old vs. young; racism, sexism, religions, and especially Democrat vs. Republican. The Moderate Party would be predicated on the prevention or mitigation of these conflicts, and to offering an alternative to the sterile destructive attacks of Democrats vs. Republicans. In modern America, one of the most threatening conflicts is that of "blacks vs. whites". Blacks have every right to press their interests and to seek improvement of their position in society. But they must recognize that such zeal can become excessive and lead to horrible worsening of the stability of the country. There are 42 million black citizens in the US; but there are also 280 million citizens who are not black. In advocating the best interests of blacks, attention must also be paid to the wellbeing of the 280 million.

- People, and even organizations, have strong sustained motivations, which should be supported and utilized. But if the world changes, some means must be found to get people to change with it and not cling to obsolete intents. Similarly, people tend to be cynical and to deny belief. Governments must therefore be agents to define reality, and the sense of what is right.

- Recognize the horror of the fact that lying is now almost official government policy, and "spin" is a growing political art form. In a very complex world, it almost impossible to tell what is true and what is false, especially if the government itself is deliberately masking the truth. As a part of this syndrome, governments have mastered the arts of concealment, misinformation, denial, "It wasn't me!"

- It must be recognized that inevitably, some of the power of governments will fall into the hands of people and organizations that are simply evil beyond understanding. This is true insanity.

The Moderate Party must deliberately design itself as much as possible as a coalition of interests which have their base and strength from the bottom up; from organizations dependent on individuals aligning themselves in groups which are capable of influencing major decisions and actions, often in opposition of more traditional top down political domination. What are these bottom up elements?

Long term protections must be maintained to prevent the breaking of laws by public officials, including and especially those violations are in the form of public corruption. Policies and actions must not sacrifice the general wellbeing in favor of improper institutional advantage or self-interest. Note that at its worst in 2005, Congress passed more than 11,000 earmarks. Even the Congress finally became embarrassed by widespread opposition and passed an anti-earmark law in 2011. Earmarks now? Maybe 150! Both political and managerial leaders must never be allowed to ignore evidence of failure or impropriety. It must be mandated that protective mechanisms, like auditors and inspectors be appointed and vigorously supported.

The rule of law must never be ignored, violated, or manipulated for perverse motives. But one of the most fundamental and cherished concepts advocated for a government is that "rightness" should be defined by "the rule of law" as stated in constitutions, enacted laws, the enduring structure of the national justice system, a body of common laws and precedents, and a legal structure of governments in which powers and authorities are both authorized and limited. Citizen's rights are protected, and their obligations defined under these laws, and usually include the right to take legal action to protect themselves. The rule of law has long been considered as the principal means by which governments are kept within proper limits. The rule of law is intended to state those roles of government that citizens will accept, and to define what governments may or may not do. In the classic dictionary sense, the rule of law is defined as "A set of substantive legal principles and laws; and the concept of the supremacy of regular, as opposed to arbitrary power; the exercise of those powers by those in authority; the doctrine that any person is subject to the ordinary laws of the region. The doctrine states that the generally constitutional legal principles are the result of judicial decisions determining the rights of private individuals in the courts.

In most countries, there has been the warm and comfortable feeling that if only the rule of law is followed, all will be well. Perhaps the greatest source for the accretion of power has come through the philosophy that the good of the individual must be subordinated to the "good of the State", and that only the state is capable of defining its own good. The right of defining the good of the state is thus reserved (usurped) by the government. Such definitions are almost always framed by some doctrine that is elaborated, defended, and rigidly enforced. In so many cases, this defining doctrine is one calling for a centrist concentration of power, and that can be exercised for any purpose and without serious restraint. Restraint mechanisms, where in use, are viewed by the tyrant as threats which must be eliminated, frustrated, subverted, or co-opted.

Second, even where there is a substantial framework for the rule of law, those mechanisms can be perverted because they rest on the often invalid assumption that the laws themselves are good and proper. This has been largely true in the United States and in most other developed countries, but it is increasingly apparent that keeping the laws good and proper is an enormously complex and sophisticated process. In many countries, rules of law and the mechanisms to protect them do not exist or are not strong enough. Thus, laws themselves are perverted and made to work against the very people they are supposed to protect. Anything – any pathological, corrupt, perverse, outrageous and dysfunctional thing – can and has been made legal and the law of the land. Pathological politics has proved time and time again that it can frustrate the intent of the rule of law and turn it upside down. It is the thesis of this book that the Moderate Party will draw government organizations back from the pernicious influence of special interests in the political system. Where the leadership is incapable or unwilling to admit and correct mistakes either to avoid negative political consequences or to conceal incompetence or corruption, The Moderate Party would have to provide a very different kind of political organization from the weak and equivocating versions from which we suffer. Common sense and courage!

Third, where the rule of law is persistently and deliberately ignored, violated, or manipulated for perverse motives, or where the professional knowledge about "how to do it right". The Moderate Party would have to stand strongly for all elements of government to face up to the responsibility to act both legally and properly, and again, the greatest ally can be the public attitude to see the party as the guardians of proper governance.

Fourth, there is a growing sense that the huge body of public regulations issued by governments has, either deliberately or incompetently, become oppressive, excessive and/or unfairly, ineptly or corruptly enforced. Here, the very concept of moderation is involved. The political system sometimes thinks that high volume, high visibility action is popular and the way to win votes. But it seems finally true that the general public has grown wiser and has begun to recognize that such excesses are both dysfunctional and wrong. Let us be cool, and learn both moderation, common sense, and the ability to get along and to collaborate instead of to hate.

Fifth, where corruption is widespread, and efforts to prevent or cure it are deliberately or incompetently inadequate. This is one of the greatest problems of governance. Corruption is in one sense, just one of the worst elements of human beings. In government, it is universal and ubiquitous. It is so unfailingly popular because it is so often spectacularly successful. Most dictators also find ways to reduce the effectiveness of governance in rooting it out. But for the general public, it is an unmitigated outrage; our money stolen, and in your face! There would be no greater obligation, and more valuable way to serve the public than for the Moderate Party to be the new, bold enemy of public corruption.

Sixth, where the control of money – both revenues and expenditures – is deliberately or incompetently vague, inadequate or obscured and where adequate preventive measures for financial management have not been developed. But this is a lot more important than simple bookkeeping, or even accounting. It is a lack of discipline in creating the hundreds of sources for expenditure – it is the legal demand for financing of programs that inflates the books. The backers of these hundreds of programs press for more money, the political leaders comply, and control is a word that never gets uttered. The Moderate Party should be smart enough to attack the real problem of financial management – too many politically mandated demands.

It is very important for the Moderate Party to see to it that the body of regulations of the government is never, either deliberately or incompetently, allowed to become oppressive, excessive and/or unfairly, ineptly or corruptly enforced. The world has become enormously complex, confusing, sophisticated. It is astonishing to realize that the population of the world has surged enormously and rapidly, and it now exceeds 7.6 billion people. By 2030, it is estimated to rise to 8.5 billion, and by 2050 to 9.7 billion, with the U. S. population, now 328 million, will rise up to about 355 million. Everything in the world, starting with the nature of these billions of human beings is inherently in conflict. This complexity involves the economy, politics, the social context, and the pressures of policies and concepts of religion, nationalism, cultural and tribal mores, all of which are in conflict with themselves and with each other, and it is in danger of becoming so complex that it simply overpowers our government systems. Every government in history has been largely managed from the top down – even the U. S. and its representative democracy. But governance is of such great complexity that little can be really "managed". In fact, there has been a very important fact: the failure of top down control by elitists. Yet it is an eternal conflict between the need for service and the exercise of power. One of the most compelling ideas is simply to reduce the range of political power. But the question of what should be the range and scope of public power is at the heart of most governments today. Not everything in our society needs to be made political. Even if one believes in the necessity of a strong political system, it is still possible to accept that politics has its limits, and that a good argument can be made for a "de minimus" government that does all of the right things (and none of the wrong things) and stays out of affairs where it is not competent.

To understand the importance of this issue, it is important to emphasize once again the surge of State Socialism and its subsequent decline. One of the crucial lessons learned is that State Socialism was based on totally dominant top down elitist control; and that fairly rapidly, its record was ultimately one of substantial and universal decline in countries all over the world. The Democratic Socialist Association (DSA) is probably largest socialist political group in the United States. It advocates the abolition of capitalism, universal government Medicare; the creation of a public banking system, eliminating "Wall Street"; the strong support of "the worker" and unions; the elimination of prisons; almost unlimited immigration and refugee inflows, no separation of parents and children, and the maintenance of sanctuary cities. But it is a very important point to realize that most of this Socialist agenda, when extensively adopted in many governments around the world, proved to be failures, and that instead of encouraging freedom and individuality, it produced some of the most vicious top down governments ever seen. The Moderate Party must understand this fact of history, and vigorously oppose the influence of so called "democratic socialism" in the U. S.

We need to be realistic in understanding our national priorities. First and foremost is human wellbeing; then we need to seek societal/national wellbeing; next then might be political/religious theories; then the functioning of governments. Political parties cannot and should not ever be seen as top priority. Human well-being should be built around certain American "core" values: observance of the Constitution; respect for human decency; integrity; honesty; accountability; leadership; responsibility; equality under the law. The emergence of American "nationalism" was critical and fundamental, but it is now being opposed for two reasons; first, it is argued as elitist and against individualism. Second, it denies the concept of "internationalism" which is seen as an inevitable tide. But much of this argumentation centers around socialist theory, which is really a more intense form of state control.

A further element of the discussion about "core values" centers around the whole complex concept of freedom of speech. The Moderate Party must defend that right even if their utterances are vicious, spiteful, false, intolerant, lying, insulting, dehumanizing, irresponsible, or just plain wrong and stupid. But is it not also true that the government has a responsibility to prevent speech that is treasonous, seditious, intolerant, inflammatory?

One of the most compelling approaches to the restraint of centrist authoritarian governments is to press for the devolution or delegation of authority over many government programs to regional (e. g. states, provinces) governments or to municipalities. There is a continuing debate about the kinds and levels of decentralization and devolution in governments; the main basis for this debate is the overwhelming fear of centrist power. The central government is in charge of this debate and has tended to act always to guarantee its own power. Cities are de facto sources of power, and they will be the main sources of leverage for local government authority. The most uncertain element in this debate is about what power should be given to regions. Typically, the strongest views against devolution come from the centrist power holders, and from macroeconomists who believe that economic development is best when driven from the top. There is also a strong element of simple inertia, in part because many do not want to change the current allocation of power because they fear or do not understand what to replace it with, and distinct tendency in every political system to face up to such challenges and the need to do some heavy lifting in the face of substantial opposition. What are the best arguments for devolution or decentralization?

1. Sharing power promotes democracy because it is easier for citizens and organizations to reach and influence local governments. Especially with social services programs, most national governments are seen as remote and preoccupied with broader issues. Decentralization also enhances the total cadre of public leadership.

2. Local governments offer the potential of achieving higher public service effectiveness and responsiveness, and of creating a better and more capable public service because it enhances the quality of local leadership. In general, local administration of public programs is seen as more practical and less theoretical or doctrinaire. Program success is more likely to be evaluated in terms of how well the public is actually served.

3. Devolution will take power out of the hands of centrist elites, reduce elitist collusion and the power of centrist agencies, and reduce the range of public activities that are vulnerable to corrupt control. It also importantly shifts the attention of special interest lobbying

groups from a single federal government target to a variety of local governments, more attuned to the general public interest.

4. As more power and authority is decentralized, it makes the relationship between the central government and local governments more balanced, since these relationships will be more often negotiated rather than dictated. Regional governments have roles to play which are genuinely regional in nature – for example, regional road nets, the allocation of land uses, the provision of public utilities or the priorities between conflicting demands on government. But to achieve these advances, regional and municipal governments must be independent and not just administrative units of the central government.

5. There is even a valid line of argument that says that regional governments are also good economic development tools. At the very least, it can be argued that a wiser allocation of scarce government resources is an economic advantage, and that local governments will be smarter about how to improve the value and performance of local economies. But the stronger argument centers on the capacity of regional governments to pursue regional economic development. The 50 American states all feel free to pursue economic development programs with international outreach. In some of the smarter countries in E. Europe, privatization and the revitalization of a private sector economy has often been delegated to regional governments freed from the straight jacket of central economic command and control. It is a wise policy to allow local governments freedom to initiate their own economic development strategies, plans and objectives, and to control the collection of whatever funds are required to carry out their own objectives rather than those of the central government. As local governments assume more control of their own economic fate, this enhances the likelihood that eventually, they will be able to free themselves from the power of central government funding. This means that decentralization or devolution must be accompanied by the courage to a shift from national funding sources to local taxation powers.

6. Part of the rethinking of the roles of local governments will involve the relationship between regional and municipal governments. In some cases, states may share some of the burden of financing key urban based social programs. In other cases, states may assume primary responsibility for some programs such as highway construction and

maintenance, universities, some parts of the health care system or parts of welfare program financing.

The ability of each public program to be effective is very much bound up in the nature of the law that creates it, since political reality seems to be that once a public program is created, it is exceedingly hard to change. It must be gotten right in the first place. Program definition is almost always highly political, and often very much a form of special interest politics, with the general public interest tends to get lost in the shuffle. Therefore, one of the prime targets for the Moderate Parry is to keep a sharp eye on the business of legislative drafting as it relates to the design of public programs. What would really be desirable in fact is to draft legislation designing public programs that is "corruption proof". Each law should state not only what authority is being created, but what authority is specifically denied. All laws should be written to make it clear that recipients of public contracts, grants, licenses, or access to public facilities must open their books to government auditors on demand.

One of the most difficult aspects of both politics and government performance is the disparity between the expressed purposes of public programs and the lack of will of the political leadership to provide the money to achieve those purposes. It is easy to understand why poor countries have great difficulty obtaining the funds to carry out programs, but this simply makes it more important to avoid making political promises that can't be kept, and makes it necessary to estimate at the time of authorization the costs of implementing each program. Failing deliberately to face up to this dilemma is a sign of pathological intent.

Another powerful line of reasoning in the design of public programs is to try and take the "money" out of special interest politics. This concept goes far beyond the narrow questions of political contributions, and must be applied to the design of hundreds of public programs. A good example is the critical importance of using open and visible competition for government contracts – as opposed to awarding contracts through political influence.

Another example might be the strict and continuous application of a general philosophy and policy not to pay any government subsidy to any profit-making organization, including "tax breaks" concealed in the national tax code.

Yet another example would be to limit eligibility for public funds to the truly needy, and not permit eligibility to extend to people who can take care of themselves. The concept should be established that since public funds will always be limited and scarce, they must be allocated as a scarcity and not as the distribution of plenty. Thus, national interests must be made to compete for such allocations, and a public record established that the funds are going to the neediest, or those who can make the highest and best use of them. Two powerful examples: social security funds can and should be limited to the poorest and not to those who chose not to provide for their own retirement; and student loans should be limited to the most needy and not distributed to families who can provide for their own children's higher education.

Legislation should be deliberately written so as to limit subsequent political interference in the drafting of public regulations, and managerial decisions implementing public programs. Many such protections are already written into public laws. Failure occurs when these limits are ignored or gamed. One powerful example has been the political attempts to control the award of public contracts, where "who do you know" substitutes for "how well can you perform". The conflict between politics vs. management pervades the whole structure of public management.

Still another approach would be to make more forms of special interest preference illegal. This has successfully been done in such areas as patronage, nepotism, non-competitive contracting, prevention of low interest loans.

Another way is to make public services that favor specific groups subject to the concept of user fees. For example, the U. S. Coast Guard conducts ice breaking operations in the Great Lakes. While this may benefit "commerce" generally, it specifically benefits shippers and ship operators who do not have to pay for their own ice breaking. The Coast Guard could continue to provide the service, but could at least charge a user fee to recoup the expenses of the government.

Another way to mitigate special interest politics is to try and modify the political system itself. Examples are term limits; the enforced transparency of government activities; requirements for public review and comment of proposed public actions such as major policies or regulations. In legislation or rules, there could be enforced publication of all groups or persons who submitted or reviewed and commented on proposals and drafts, or who attended meetings in which legislation was modified. In addition, special analyses could be mandated for publication evaluating all instances where special advantages are created, and who would benefit and how – the ancient test of who benefits and who is harmed. In most governments, the government itself refuses to provide such analyses, but it is seen as crucial information by media people and public interest groups. Even though this provision would be hard to enforce, such a law would lay down a legal basis of fact that could be investigated. This might act to limit back room interventions, since a post audit could catch those who failed to disclose their interventions, or failed to report honestly in official documents – in a manner similar to post audits of tax returns. Laws could be modified to create penalties for "undue influence" in the decisions creating public authority. In other words — Welcome to the Moderate Party.

THE "RULE OF LAW" AND WHY IT IS NOT ENOUGH

One of the most fundamental and cherished concepts advocated for any government is that "rightness" should be defined by "the rule of law": that is, the basic design and operation of governments as stated in constitutions, enacted laws, the enduring structure of the national justice system, a body of common laws and precedents, and a legal structure of governments in which powers and authorities are both authorized and limited. Citizen's rights are protected, and their obligations defined under these laws, and usually include the right to take legal action to protect themselves. The rule of law has long been considered as the principal means by which governments are kept within proper limits. The rule of law is intended to state those roles of government that citizens will accept, and to define what governments may or may not do. In the classic dictionary sense, the rule of law is defined as "1. A set of substantive legal principles and laws; 2. The concept of the supremacy of regular, as opposed to arbitrary power; 3. The exercise of those powers by those in authority; 4. The doctrine that any person is subject to the ordinary laws of the region; and 5. The doctrine that the generally constitutional legal principles are the result of judicial decisions determining the rights of private individuals in the courts.

In most countries, there has been the warm and comfortable feeling that if only the rule of law is followed, all will be well. Perhaps the greatest source for the accretion of power has come through the philosophy that the good of the individual must be subordinated to the "good of the State", and that only the state is capable of defining its own good. The right of defining the good of the state is thus reserved (usurped) by the government. Such definitions are almost always framed by some doctrine that is elaborated, defended, and rigidly enforced. In so many cases, this defining doctrine is one calling for a centrist concentration of power, and that can be exercised for any purpose and without serious restraint. Restraint mechanisms, where in use, are viewed by the tyrant as threats which must be eliminated, frustrated, subverted, or co-opted.

Second, even where there is a substantial framework for the rule of law, those mechanisms can be perverted because they rest on the often invalid assumption that the laws themselves are good and proper. This has been largely true in the United States and in most other developed countries, but it is increasingly apparent that keeping the laws good and proper is an enormously complex and sophisticated process. In many countries, rules of law and the institutions mechanisms to protect them do not exist or are not strong enough. Thus, laws themselves are perverted and made to work against the very people they are supposed to protect. Anything – any pathological, corrupt, perverse, outrageous and dysfunctional thing – can and has been made legal and the law of the land. Pathological politics has proved time and time again that it can frustrate the intent of the rule of law and turn it upside down.

THE MODERATE PARTY AGENDA

1. It is vital and fundamental that the Party is always seen as advocating and supporting what is considered the "core values" of American society, seen as respect for each other, the respect for human decency, self-reliance, integrity, honesty, accountability, responsibility, leadership, and equality under the law. Seek always to tell the truth between the American public and its government.
2. Add to this the core principles of government by the Moderate Party: moderation, common sense, and courage.
3. The heart of policy should always be to act mainly in the interests of the general public, and firmly to reject the improper grip of special interest politics.
4. Do not pit one element of American society against another. The strength of the Party will be to be able to forge collaboration and cooperation, even among groups and people who think differently.

5. Freedom of speech is vital; but it is more than talking loud. Who talks loud today? Everybody!

6. As a nation, we have provided ourselves with hundreds of thousands of laws, regulations and administrative procedures. The great mass and complexity of these instruments of government has become a threat, and it must become an objective of the Party to simplify and ease the burden of their application back to that which is really essential.

7. In addition, the dynamics of adding to these instruments will continue, and thus the Party must keep stringent control of the drafting and application of new laws and regulations.

8. The Moderate Party must do something that almost no government has ever done fully successfully: keep itself essentially free of government corruption.

9. Through it all — there must be a compelling attention to the care of the truly needy in our society, and it is proper for the government to provide what these people cannot.

10. And the American public has every right to expect its government to function with high effectiveness, doing the right things in the right way.

DEVELOPMENT OF THE NATIONAL ECONOMY

The following represent the most important motivations—good and bad—for undertaking major transformations of a national economy:

1. Move up from an agrarian economy.
2. Force the pace of economic development.
3. Diversify the economy. Often, this has meant denying the agriculture sector resources in order to finance strategies elsewhere in the economy.
4. Break down class structures; create a larger more powerful middle class.
5. Build national strength and military support. This usually involves creation of a form of "military-industrial complex" which gives the military greater leverage over elements of the economy, and generally exempts it from full accountability and even civilian scrutiny.
6. Break free from external "colonialism"
7. Protect/develop infant industries.
8. Constrain improper actions of the private sector by control or regulation.
9. Fix gaps in the economy left by the normal evolution of the private sector.
10. Share—or assume—the large investment costs when the private sector cannot.

11. Nagative use of State Owned Enterprises (SOEs) as a source of political patronage and corruption.
12. Greater control of productive resources as a source of public revenue.
13. Doctrinal resistance to the investment of foreign capital. In some cases, the nationalization of foreign properties led to creation of SOEs.
14. Use of parastatal institutions to provide "business management" of public infrastructure and services (i.e. insurance, health care, etc.)
15. Gain control of development financing.
16. Provide guaranteed financial backing (i.e. "full faith and credit") for international loans. Use external capital to finance industrial expansion at a greater (usually excessive) rate, while using domestic revenues for social programs.
17. Take over failed private enterprises.
18. Create competition for monopolistic private sector situations.
19. Stem capital flight.
20. Reallocate investments by sector.
21. Build up workforce intensive industry; avoid "exportation" of jobs. But there is a nasty track record in many countries of excessive redundancy, low labor productivity, large inflationary wage settlements, politically powerful unions, etc.
22. But perhaps the most important of all: to create the resources to pay for vital support of human needs.

Then, here is a list of key economic issues that the noted economist Samuelson sees as crucial to economic improvement:

- The advance of information technology as both an economic boon as a new employer. The shift in the nature of jobs and economies.
- The intractable nature of the US governments budget deficits, including the concepts around SIP.
- General high public and private debt. The concern that the tax system needs major renovation.
- The rise of China; the challenge of Chinese economic policy approaches compared to the Western model
- The real issue of income inequality and the need for a living wage. Is it morally justified for Warren Buffett to have $31 billion?
- The dilemma of immigration and refugees

- An aging population, and the changing demands on social services.
- Globalization; what does it really mean, and how far will it go?
- Urbanization
- The shift in worker protection from unions to employers, and the government.

The overwhelming public policy objective must be this: to recognize the great expansion of the American population (now 328 million of us), and the growing complexity of American society, its growing sophistication, and the level of people's expectations, and to design a government and an economy capable of dealing with this complexity.

Union membership is down from 30% of workers in the 50's to 11% today. Further, the private sector membership is down to just 7%, and it is the public sector with membership of about 34% that is the real current strength of the union movement. This decline reflects the shifting nature of the workforce, and the fact that employers have figured out that if they provide vital support and benefits, to their workers, the need for union representation is vastly reduced. In general, union leaders are all committed to the heavy linkage to the Democratic Party, and this is especially true among teachers and other public sector workers. Governments are increasingly responsive to the value of providing more specific and targeted employment training, tuned to actual economic realities and needs. These kinds of programs need not be very expensive, and they can be made more responsive to disparities faced by minorities and women. And they are almost certain to include heavy emphasis on the popular virtues of the work ethic of "earn your way" It is estimated that 40% or more of job seekers are single mothers.

A further, and compellingly important element is to strengthen the power and independence of the private sector, and indeed there is a tide running, in the decline of state socialism, that is enabling exactly that. The collateral is then to limit the powers of the central government versus the private sector. It is increasingly being recognized that governments are surprisingly ill equipped to manage the operational levels of the economy, and that the private sector is far superior in these skills. There does not seem to be any standard universal definition of what should be done by the government and what should be kept in the hands of private interests, but the following is reasonably accepted:

A. Roles that should be performed mainly by the national government:

* Welfare insurance

* National defense
* National security and justice system
* Certain kinds of regulation
* Government-to-government international relations
* National laws; maintenance of the Constitution
* Certain national transportation systems
* Certain environmental protections

B. Roles that are better performed mainly by local government:

* Elementary/secondary education
* Urban services and infrastructure (e. g. water Supply, sewage, trash disposal, streets, etc.)
* Parks, recreational and cultural facilities
* Welfare assistance
* Housing – public
* Power sources policy and regulation

C. Roles that can/should be shared with the private sector:

* Environmental protection
* Highways and public infrastructure
* Natural resources development and management
* Power generation and transmission
* Transportation: rail, road systems, airports, etc.
* Manufacturing: "national" industries vs. open industries
* Universities and training
* Entertainment
* Housing for most citizens
* Utilities ownership and/or operation

D. Roles that should be performed just the private sector:

* All other manufacturing
* Consumer consumption
* Agriculture and food distribution

The Moderate Party would pursue a policy of trade promotion rather than trade prevention. In the United States, the private sector is perfectly capable of pursuing highly effective economic development.

All too often, government involvement is seen as improper subsidizing of private companies. Take for example this gem from current US agricultural policy. The USDA Market Access Program provides farmers with money grants, low interest loans, (often forgiven), loan guarantees, subsidized insurance and "market access" grants to food producers to support food exporting, including money for foreign advertising and access help. What producers have been helped?

Almonds	Blueberrys
Apples	Confections
Asparagus	Cotton
Beans	Cranberrys
Beer	Dairy products
Grapes	Pistacios
Honey	Popcorn
Hops	Poultry
Kiwis	Potatos
Live stock	Prunes
Mohair	Raisins
Oranges	Seafood
Papaya	Soybeans
Paper products	Sunflowers
Papaya	Tomatos
Peanuts	Walnuts
Pears	Watermelons
Pet foods	Wheat
Wine	

The point of this tedious list is deliberate: everybody can use special interest politics to get money or preferment from the federal government. Everybody. And if anybody gets funding, then everybody gets funding. Government funds are paid to trade associations, commissions, institutes, councils, boards, departments, international groups, coalitions, bureaus, federations or just plain companies. If cotton or tobacco gain preferment, can raisins and aspargus be far behind? In fact, the raisin guys are not behind at all. The raisin lobby has already taken $ 38 million out of the public purse to pay for its overseas marketing. (Bingman, "Government From the Bottom Up").

Large special lending institutions lent money for farm investments, operations, and even home loans – often at borrowing rates below the normal lending market. Additional subsidies came in the form of cheap electrical power or fuels, rural telephone development, special subsidies in the tax structure, and finally in direct subsidies to farmers as a form of welfare or in the name of income maintenance. But despite several decades of such support, the numbers of farms has continued to decline and this remains a hot political issue. The pathology is that governments have continued to subsidize agriculture despite the very obvious changes in the realities of agribusiness. The 'small farmer" is out, andd big agribusiness is very much in. Government efforts to help the small farmer often fly in the face of this economic reality, and have succeeded in skewing the market, and keeping agriculture protected from true market tests.

Agriculture remains a political hot spot for two main reasons: a lingering and emotional concern for the small farmer; and the special interest politics of agribusiness. To quote James Bovard about the U. S. experience in the 1980's, "Prosperity is created through organized scarcity" and this has often been the goal of many United States Department of Agriculture (USDA) farm programs. The USDA rewarded farmers for not planting 78 million acres of farm land. Government shut down some of the best farm land in order to limit supply and drive up world corn and wheat prices. But each time Congress has driven up American crop prices above world prices, American farmers were driven out of the world market. Thanks to political mismanagement, one of America's leading industries is becoming a ball-and-chain on the American economy. Further, to quote the Washington Post (June 30, 2018) "Inevitably the farm bill showers benefits on well-to-do business owners who don't need or deserve taxpayer help." Congress showered agribusiness with taxpayer largess as an aggressive form of corporate welfare, even when incomes reached an all-time high a half-decade ago. The reality is that when the whole income picture for farmers is considered, farm households earn about $119,880 per year, compared to the average income of households generally which was $79,265. Included in farm income numbers is income earned from non-farm work, and capital increases in land and property value. It would surely be one of the priority arenas of concern for the Moderate Party to undertake a total redesign of our whole obsolete catering to agriculture special interests

But at another level, the U. S. government extends this kind of perverse relationship all over the federal government budget. It is infamously known for a form of public budgeting widely known as "PORK", which is closely linked to another budget skill known as "EARMARKS", which is closely followed by the friendly process of "LOGROLLING". These are the tools of special interest politics. Pork means the ability of special interests politics to slip provisions in bills passed by legislatures which favor their own advantage, either in the form of money or in some form of favoritism or special advantage. Earmarks are funds set aside by legislators for specific organizations or activities favored by some politician: roads, or schools, or clients or "community development". These mechanisms are perverse in the sense that they substitute corrosive political preferment for national or superior decisions. As a current 2017 example, as Congress strives mightily to pass a tax reform bill, there is a move to include in such a bill a provision that would open up about 800,000 acres of land in Alaska to new oil drilling; totally irrelevant but advocated because it supposedly provide some more jobs and — income for oil companies.

According to the Congressional Research Service, there were 4155 earmarks in 1991. By 2002, that number had increased to 10,631; and by 2015 it had surged to 11,772 items. These assaults on the federal budget had become so frequent and so easy to get and so very expensive that even the U. S. Congress was driven to act. In 2011, a new law for an "earmark" moratorium" was enacted, and the results were remarkable. It is estimated that earmarks now total fewer than 200; but those that are passed are still very expensive. Citizens Against Government Waste has estimated that Congress has still "snuck in" some $4.2 billion of questionable expenditures. And wait 'til next year or so.

Another serious economic debate is that about whether governments should be actively involved in what are called "Anti-trust" laws and programs. This is an ancient issue, which began as early as the 1870's, involving emerging super tycoons like John D. Rockefeller, Andrew Carnegie, J. P. Morgan, "Commodore Vanderbilt, Henry Flagler, and in another arena, William Randolph Hearst. The ability of these men to capture so much of the national wealth and to create threatening monopolies of power produced a powerful national reaction which led to antitrust moves such as the Sherman Antitrust Act in 1890, the Clayton Antitrust Act of 1914, the creation of the Federal

Trade Commission, and hundreds of laws and regulations designed to prevent the accretion of monopoly power. It should be remembered that "antitrust" also includes protection against market allocation, bid rigging, price fixing, cartels, monopolies, bid suppression, and improper mergers and acquisitions, both vertical and horizontal. These fears continue to this day, and the Moderate Party would certainly seek to revitalize modern protective laws and to galvanize the American population to once again resist any threats of overwhelming private company power. The conflict is this: how do we allow the government to protect us when necessary without allowing an excess of government control?

A major economic policy goal is national job creation and upgrading. How would this be done? First, the basic need is an economy that is expanding enough to create sufficient employment demands to absorb the increase in population, which creates the need for jobs. In many countries that created Socialist economies, the bitter lesson learned was that most of them were seriously dysfunctional and had to be replaced. Since the nature of jobs has changed from muscle to brain, the training of people coming into the workforce must reflect the change. Some of the change needs to be reflected in the nature of the national education system both through schools and also through employers who are willing to train their employees on the job. Part of this new understanding reflects the fact that there are now 6.7 million unfilled jobs in the economy, and the prime-age employment rate has returned to a near-peak 79.3%. It should be clear that we must understand what skills these jobs require, to make sure that we are providing the right training.

An important potential lies in the willingness of the government and private sector employers to raise the minimum wage. The reality now is that the federal minimum wage of $7.25 per hour has largely been overtaken by events. While Congress has lacked the courage to raise the minimum, states and other local governments have acted more forcefully. According to a study from the University of California Labor Center, 44 major cities have established their own minimum wage levels, and at least 20 states have also raised their pay level bottoms. The average pay of minimum wage workers has risen to about 57% of the national median wage. Unions, employers and huge numbers of workers themselves are now heavily pushing the Congress to find its courage and raise the federal minimum wage for all.

But by far the most important evolution in the American workforce is the surging roles of women. This is not just a "numbers" change. This is the whole broadening and deepening and enrichment of the range of positions that women are filling, and the exceptional upgrading of the capacity by which they achieve such skills

In very complex ways, the nature of the American workforce is linked to the nature of the world economy. There are slow but enormous tides running which can both enhance and inhibit the nature of the workforce tides. Part of this problem has become the rise in the movement of immigrant (legal and illegal) into the country, but also the rise of the wave of refugees attempting to enter. The U. S. has a long and enviable record of allowing and even encouraging the entry of immigrants, and these people have an extraordinary record of rapid and productive integration into the American society. The fear about refugees centers around their illegal and aggressive status, uncertainty about their ability to be absorbed, and the very bad elements like drug dealers, criminals, and MS-13 gang members who poisoning public acceptance.

Thus, there is a wide and very interesting range of positive policies that can be supported by the Moderate Party to enhance the effectiveness of job creation and the overall quality of the American work. One of the newest and most interesting assessments is the supposed emergence of "Age of the Robot" where we will all be happily replaced by machines and will no longer have to work at all. But realistically, there are whole classes of human effort that are beyond robots: the astonishing range and impact of human minds. And one also wonders about – waiters and sales clerks and doctors and nurses and artists and musicians and actors, and many forms of arcane human interrelationships. Automation can speed action, reduce errors, reduce costs, deal with the most complex mechanics, and even reduce human boredom. But there is perhaps still more than 50% of jobs that demand "thinking." Education is vital; the nature of work demands has shifted from shovels and production lines in factories, where automation has displaced so many workers, to offices, schools, stores, and other occupations with a need for higher levels of intellectual preparation. Part of the fears arising from illegal immigration is that the people coming in are uneducated, lack the ability to fill jobs with substantial education demands, and will not find the production jobs of the past. American society is making progress in relation to female and minority workers; not just a demand equality, but a search for advancement. There is a feeling that high schools and colleges must offer courses that are more realistically attuned to actual workplace needs.

Unionism can and should be revitalized, but it must be made to return to its roots and become once again the representative of the interests of workers, and not just a political prop for the Democratic Party. Union membership is down from about 30% of workers in the 50's, to about 11% today. Most union members now are in the public sector – about 34% of government workers. In the private sector, this number is a measly 7%. Employers have learned to create good on-the-job working conditions, and the provision of social services such as health insurance and retirement programs. As this has happened, the value of unions as worker protectors has drastically declined.

Recently, the Supreme Court ruled out mandatory dues collection from non-union members. A telling example of the consequences of this change is typified by such an action enacted in the state of Wisconsin in 2011. The change cost teachers unions one half of their membership and two thirds of their dues income. It is therefore feared that, nationally, the Supreme Court decision will cost unions one third of their members, which would be especially compelling in the public unions, which are heavily political and dedicated supporters of the Democratic Party. Worker disappointment with this kind of political favoritism has been a cause for some union membership decline. Unions still work when they go back to their roots and work to serve their membership.

THE INFORMAL ECONOMY

The informal economy is defined by De Soto as "the refuge of individuals who find that the costs of abiding by existing laws in the pursuit of legitimate economic objectives exceeds the benefits. It is essential that the state remember that before it can distribute the nation's wealth, the must *produce* wealth. And that in order to produce wealth it is necessary that the state's actions not obstruct the actions of its citizens, who, after all, know better than anyone what they want and what they have to do. The state must restore it its citizens the right to take on productive tasks, a right that it has been usurping and obstructing. The state must limit itself to functioning in those necessary areas in which private industry cannot function. This does not mean that the state will wither away and die."

A distinction is usually made between the informal economy and the so called "underground" economy which is broader and includes illegal activities such as drugs, prostitution, illegal betting and smuggling. The informal economy is not confined to poor countries, and in fact every country has a substantial informal sector in its economy. However, the size and variety of the informal economy is directly related to the capacity of a national economy to generate enough economic strength to support its people. When the formal economy is too weak, people often have no option but to enter the informal economy as a means of survival. One of the pathologies of many governments is that they fail to recognize this reality, and view the informal economy as a form of crime, often called a "black market" existing only to avoid taxes and escape regulations. In truth, in many countries the informal economy is saving the country from economic collapse. The government can and does use laws and police enforcement to suppress the informal economy even when it knows that it provides employment and income that the state has failed to provide.

There are no barriers to entry into the informal economy. Anybody capable of performing a service or providing a good can become a provider. The most likely types of work in the informal economy are casual laborers, construction workers, and personal services providers such as servants, janitors, trash collectors, porters, messengers, errand runners, delivery people, child care providers, street vendors, and even panhandlers. In addition, if some capital is available, other people may be able to become small retailers or customer service providers. One of the most frequent such service is transportation in urban areas where networks of jitney cars and minivans supplement scarce and inadequate public transportation. Small scale manufacturing is widespread, including the fine arts of making cheap copies of Gucci handbags and Omega watches. Many crafts are represented, including carpenters, plumbers, masons, electricians, tailors, and auto mechanics, and many of these entrepreneurs are capable of working in both the formal and informal economies at the same time, depending on what work is available.

The informal economy has many obvious downsides. First, while the activities are all legal in the formal sense, they are illegal when they escape the tax collection system and avoid government regulation. Their small scale of operations often prevents them from economies of scale and mostly they must refrain from some management practices like advertising or internet linkages that can be traced. In many cases, there are added costs of business for bribing the police, or to buying off inspectors. Property ownership is also dangerous, and thus the protection of physical facilities is difficult. Informal operators may be the victims of thieves and protection rackets since it is difficult to appeal for police protection. There is seldom any real job security, work may be uncertain, income and wages are often unstable and fluctuating since most informal activities are highly competitive, with too many workers seeking too few jobs. Few work benefits such as health care or unemployment compensation are possible. But surprisingly, wages in the informal sector often compare favorably with those in the formal economy, where the excess of workers also keeps wages down.

Finally, economic development has been remarkably muddled through the emergence of an exceptional proposal entitled "The Green New Deal" which is said to be motivated by plans to reduce energy consumption to "zero emission" by 2030. At this point, it is simply a vague and unexplained dream, or as the Economist puts it, "the outline of a sketch". It insists on the compelling necessity to save the planet by reducing energy consumption, especially in energy production from fossil fuels, the elimination of 253 million private cars and 133 million trucks that burn carbon fuels, along with the restructuring of most industries, and the forced reconstruction of 130 million private residences. The concept then subsumes dozens of political socialist issues not related to energy: unemployment, Medicare for All, free college education, free child care, universal income, and reparations for former slavery. The cost? Somewhere between $ 2 trillion and $ 14 trillion.

But its advocates are all but silent on the overwhelming importance of nuclear energy as potentially the greatest carbon-free source of power, and it is virtually silent on the real problem which is not in consumption but through the fundamental reduction on the generation of carbon itself. The carbon tax is being tested, but the real promise seems to be the emergence, rather rapidly of new and more powerful technologies that dispose of the carbon dioxide itself in much more effective ways.

THE MODERATE PARTY AGENDA

1. One of the most important policies that the Party must undertake is somehow to design a national economy capable of supporting a rapidly increasing and a far more complex and sophisticated population now exceeding 328 million people.
2. We must understand the lessons learned from the world-wide failures of State Socialism and resist its role in the U. S. in favor of a market-based competitive economy.
3. As a collateral to this, it would be perfectly proper for governments to maintain relationships with the private sector that rely on collaboration and coordination, and not on conflict and opposition.

4. The reputation around the economic world is the repeated failure of policies of import substitution and prevention, and the lack of export promotion, and these policies should be stoutly resisted.

5. It is time to draw governments back from their long-term subsidies for agriculture and rural development, since these elements of the country have evolved to the point that they can manage and finance their own affairs.

6. One of the worst failings of our political system is the bitter fact of political preferment. The Moderate Party must be capable and willing to do away with the perverse political sins of "pork", and "earmarking" and "log-rolling", and all of the other forms of political preferment.

7. It is widely recognized that the economy is now more reliant than ever on the decline of the shovel in the workplace, and the rise of the "brain". It is vital to support the relationships between the government and the private sector in the improving the connection between education and work.

8. Should the Moderate Party take a stand on raising the minimum wage? Yes. It should be supported.

9. As part of this line of economic reasoning, it is imperative that the Party should continue implacable and productive support of the enhancement of the roles of women and minorities, not only in the economy but in society which has vital secondary impact on the economy itself.

10. Yes, support and encourage the informal economy in the economy, and in its ability to integrate people into American society.

VITAL SOCIAL SERVICES

What is the basic obligation of governments? The answer should be cast in terms to define American society, culture, values, relationships, responsibilities as first and foremost the responsibility of our citizens themselves and the organizations and relationships we create.

This is counter to the philosophy of State Socialism which demands that life in a country should be controlled by the government. But all over the world, State Socialism has failed, or at best proved to be seriously flawed. This proves the soundness of our national thinking. The people are right; not the government. It is their lives, and they are responsible for them. Part of these lives are the fact of eternal pressures and conflicts, but this is basically HUMAN REALITY. Livelihoods have to be earned, problems must be faced, there are winners and losers, families fight, workers deal with bosses, costs go up, bills have to be paid, the home team loses.

Now, more than ever in recent years, there has been a surge in the public dialog advocating Socialist social concepts, centering around a health care system that is free or heavily subsidized; on free college education in public universities; on free child care and little or no taxation of a broad range of citizens. But the Moderate Party should stand fast in its adherence to the primary responsibility of the people themselves. Our society has survived and prospered and expanded because, in the last analysis, life's clashes can be negotiated and compromises reached, and agreement and collaboration prove superior to conflict and unreason. The governments of the U.S. can and should be scaled to fit around this great national strength of "meeting in the middle". Let there be zealots, but do not let them control. Our governments can and should be bastions for the care and support of this middle world of moderation and collaboration.

The role of the government must meet the nation's need for social services and should therefore be defined within this framework. To be explicit, the government is not responsible to provide every citizen with "cradle to grave" social services. Remember the compelling fact that State Socialism governments become heavily controlling. Government roles should be designed to supplement and support the national systems for the delivery of health care, education, social services, housing, nutrition, and ultimately for retirement and old age. And in fact, that is approximately how our world functions now in reality, and despite a few lurches and staggers, this moderate middle approach has proved effective and sturdy. Consider the fact that the government now includes substantial programs including the following:

1. Medicaid
2. Medicare
3. Special Nutritional Assistance Program
4. Cash payments
5. Housing assistance
6. Earned income tax credit
7. Relief from Federal income taxes
8. Children's aid programs
9. Etc.

But it always seems to be the case that critics persistently decry to inadequacy of this public support, and call for "more". Statistics published by the U. S. Census Bureau state that 43 million people, or 12.7% of the population earn $25,000 per year or less.

The adamant position has been so powerful that it is preventing the ability of the US government to modify, reform, or reduce any of these programs. In other words, political gridlock and lack of courage create bad management when these programs urgently need upgrading and more efficiency.

What then are the kinds of problems that need attention?

It must be constantly emphasized that people must take care of themselves, and not look to the government to provide everything. An interesting example: In Ethiopia, the government sponsors a program, called the Urban Productive Safety Net Project, in which neighborhood committees check out and then select people who warrant help who are assigned to government jobs, receive a living wage, and can obtain training to upgrade skills. This approach is deliberately intended to replace simple minded programs where anybody could get a subsidy of fixed amount forever. (Economist: 2 Jun 18).

We must resist the political and emotional extreme view that the government must always provide "more" and "all". It is merely bad, cheap politics to keep saying that government programs are never "enough", and more money is endlessly demanded. There are ideas advanced to provide every citizen with either a monthly stipend or a guaranteed annual income provided presumably by the Federal government linked with state, county and city governments. Estimates have been for monthly payments around $500 as is being paid in California, to an annual income around $30,000. Who would pay the enormous costs of such programs? "The rich". But in truth, it would require huge increases in taxation for everybody not on the dole. The United States has by various means developed a health care system, admittedly complex and often inadequate, that still manages to provide health care for all but about 8 million people, and many of those people are young and healthy and don't feel the need for health care protection. Health insurance is provided by employers for about 217 million people. Medicare covers an additional 57 million. Medicaid/Social Security provides often subsidized care for another 60 million. If there are really people without some recourse, there are possible rather modest increments of expansion of either Medicare or Medicaid that could cover them. It would be insane to destroy this existing system, creating huge problems for more than 300 million people, in order to install a whole new system run by a single government agency.

At present, more than 42 million people pay no federal income tax. Of course, the genuine poor and helpless or disadvantaged must be helped; but there is no reason that they won't be. Many social services organizations and institutions are mostly self-supporting, which is a good thing. Government help must be mostly "help." Example: there are more than 44 million people getting a SNAP food allowance. Arguments regarding the imposition of work requirements and food boxes instead of money are based on the concern about system misuse. There are other arguments that the cost of food differs from place to place, and therefore state should have more latitude to adjust benefits. There are constant concerns about the large numbers of people who cannot find employment, or that can narrowly survive only by working two jobs.

Yet, there are legitimate public policy issues to be faced. For example, many cities are "gentrifying" which is good both for life style and for the urban tax base. But it also pushes people out of areas that they could afford, so that there is now a shortage in many urban areas of housing that the poor can afford. Housing costs also go up because of the greater costs of construction or renovation, from uncaring zoning, and for the shrinking relative value of public tax funding.

But reality is that cities are almost all overwhelmed, and may not be able to deliver what is needed. Many older housing units occupied by low income people are being bought up and renovated, thus driving out the poor tenants. But the housing construction industry lacks the financial incentive to construct new low-income housing units. It is estimated that there are now about 1.56 million people who are essentially homeless, but the statistics are very confusing. About 44% of those considered homeless are employed. The rate of homeless per 10,000 population has actually declined to the point where it is the lowest on record. Most homeless are temporary "transitional" public housing. There are also said to be about 6.9 million more people who simply cannot afford adequate housing with their current income. Presidential candidate Kamala Harris has advocated creation of a national plan to provide tax credits from the federal government for people facing high rents. She would like the federal government to subsidize any housing rent which exceeds more than 30% of total household income. But the real problem is the lack of housing, and pumping up public funding by billions of dollars would simply drive up prices, and the people who really suck up the money would be landlords and tax collectors.

One of the main government instruments for helping the low-income population is the granting of tax credits which reduces loss of income in the form of those taxes. But some 44% of low-income people pay no income tax at all, so a tax credit seems like an inadequate solution. Similarly, in cities where rent controls have been acted, better off people hastened to get into rent controlled units where they can stay forever, thus again reducing the number of housing units available for the poor.

San Francisco is a powerful example. Gentrification is caused in part by the very high income level in the city, and the high income population is increasing many times faster than the provision of places to live. A one bedroom apartment is now costing more than $3400/month. Zoning laws promote the addition of new apartment housing.

Similarly, in New York City that used to brag that it had one of the best housing programs in the country, now finds itself with a program suffering from a backlog of lack of enough units, and mounting lack of adequate unit maintenance and repair. The New York Housing Authority now says it needs "a major infusion of capital, totaling around $32 billion." It says it has a waiting list of 220,000 people. Meanwhile, the rest of the city resists higher taxes, and there are growing assertions that a serious part of the NYHA is its own costly mismanagement.

Thus, while gentrification is very importantly improving the economic condition of cities, and thus has to be encouraged, there is a strong moral and public policy obligation to provide housing for the very poor. It should follow that the new better paid residents will have to part with their higher income in taxes for adequate housing provision. Some cities such as San Francisco and New York have announced that they will take care of their poor. Other residents, especially blacks, are forced to move if they can, although the lowest income families have the greatest difficulty in relocating. Unfortunately, one of the consequences of this claim is to attract poor people to move to these cities take advantage of the assistance. Gentrification also improves the availability of better paid jobs, shops, restaurants and other amenities, and to reduce some of the commuting burden, and even to reduce crime.

Another example of the value of gentrification has been in Washington, D. C. A case has been made about the impact of the new stadium built for the Washington Nationals baseball team. The whole rather run-down neighborhood near the stadium has experienced a remarkable resurgence. In an area where there had been 977 homes, there are now 3809. Income for residents in the area has risen from just over $34,000 to about $ 78,000 now. Property value in the 80's at $1.5 million are now valued at about $2.65 million. But in 2000, the population in this area was about 17,000 blacks and 18,000 whites. These numbers now are estimated to be 13,000 blacks and 47,000 whites. It is conceded that gentrification has been negative for some of the black population. While the city in total lost population up to the seventies, estimated at minus 118,000 people, the latest figures show recent gains of more than 130,000 to a new high of more than 700,000.

The Federal Housing Finance Agency (FHFA, a combination of the old Fanny May and Freddie Mac) backs mortgages valued at $5.3 billion. The argument is that this represents an excessive level of Federal government in a sector of the economy that is, and should be, between private citizens and private companies. FHFA acts like a corporation, and it earns a profit, which is seen by critics as improper. The basic issue always has been why the Federal government is so involved so deeply in the housing insurance business. The Moderate Party would retain the organization, but cut its role back to one of emergency protection.

THE MODERATE PARTY AGENGA

1. The basic principle of social service: fundamentally, people should accept the need to take care of themselves and their families, and rely on the government primarily for help and assistance.
2. Thus, the nature of social services should be based on strong ties of collaboration and cooperation in a world of moderate accommodation.
3. There must be a serious intent to avoid the political problem of inability to respond to self-serving demand for "more", but instead to set stable priorities in the allocation social services.
4. A special case has become the availability of housing in urban areas, with a special concern for the needs of the poor and unguarded.
5. A case should be made that the age of retirement should reflect the fact that people are living longer and in better health, and more than 80% see themselves as financially secure. Thus, the retirement age could safely be raised.

NATIONAL HEALTH CARE

Health care is always one of the top two or three issues with the American public because of its vital importance, its confusion and complexity and its cost. The most fundamental issue seems to be whether health care and health insurance are the moral and policy responsibilities of governments. The proper answer seems to be no; the U. S. has spent decades evolving our current system, and in fact most people seem pretty satisfied with the status quo, based largely on heath care insurance provided by employers, by the government through Medicare and Medicaid, by VA and the military, and by individual provision. But also they look at ominous intervention of government, a in the Chinese "one child" law, the mediocre performance of some of the national systems in other countries. All too often, State-run systems proved to be major sources of government domination and mismanagement. But still, polls of all kinds have shown, for 20 years or more, that 80% or more of American citizens see health care as the single most important public issue.

But simply stated, it should not be national policy to force every one of our 328 million citizens to have the most expensive possible health insurance, no matter who pays. Many people believe that the government has a moral obligation to insist that every citizen is covered. Others see another form of moral obligation which is to help people to possess the smartest policy to meet their real needs. As of now, the average annual cost of Medicaid is in excess of $6500 per person. The monthly cost of all kinds of plans is now about $495, and deductible requirements can amount to almost $5000 per year applied across all plans. Being without health insurance is not the same as being without health care. Living without health insurance is a gamble, but life is a gamble. The system should be more effectively designed to deal with unexpected medical emergencies – and then charging an appropriate fee for them. For example, a young person might go for many years without the need for medical treatment and then experience some emergency. The system should allow that person to get treatment in any emergency medical facility, but should then be expected to pay for it afterwards. Those who are really not able to pay would be treated as charity cases at public expense.

There is a fundamental difference between those who are unable to pay, and those who are unwilling to pay, for perfectly acceptable reasons. People may want to spend their money on other things. Young people, for example, should be able to decide that they can perfectly well live with no health insurance because they are young and healthy. Should such people be <u>forced</u> to pay? Lack of health protection is a risk but life is a risk. And single people should not be forced to pay for insurance to cover children or pregnancies.

In other words, the government is not the perfect solution, and it should not be allowed to overcome people's own decisions. The basic philosophy should not be "your government has mandated the optimum health insurance system", but instead should be "we will have a system that allows individuals to decide what they need and want." When the government forces the provision of unnecessarily broad and inclusive insurance, it is not benefiting citizens. It should be clearly understood that the great majority of the 180 million people insured under an employer provided plan, and another 65 million people who provided under some other private plan are, despite some glitches, satisfied with this arrangement. The government should bend its efforts to expanding the ability of businesses, especially smaller ones, to provide health care and not on destroying the capabilities that already exist. There are simple, sensible ways that the coverage of Medicaid and Medicare can be extended where necessary. The government might even want to accept the obligation to help design and implement simpler, less expensive plans.

Finally, there is the embarrassing and humiliating national record of system corruption. The Justice Department just this year has indicted more than 600 people, 165 of whom are doctors accused of creating more than $6 billion of false billings. Hundreds of doctors have been formally accused of prescribing and distributing dangerous drugs, and there have been 64,000 reputed deaths. The managers of the Medicaid program have themselves admitted that, in 2012, they allowed improper payments totaling $19.2 billion! The response? By 2015, improper payments had risen to $29 billion. The response? It is now estimated that improper payments will reach more than $ 38 billion by 2017. In addition, improper payments are also out of control in the Medicare program, totaling $41 billion. The loss of valuable funds is serious enough in itself, but it is simply incomprehensible to understand how such criminal activity goes on year after year after year.

The Moderate Party would support a simplified and modulated system of individual, public and private health insurance systems.

Changing the eligibility age for Medicaid and Medicare, and Social Security is now increasingly debated, driven by two elements. First is the fact that, slowly over time, the life span of Americans is lengthening, and as people live longer, usually in retirement, the costs of maintaining their health and wellbeing has risen. To some extent it is argued that longer lived people can also tend to work longer, and this precipitates the argument that the official age for retirement can be made later. The Moderate Party would probably accept this argument, as long as it is tied to the absolute of providing care for the truly needy.

In many countries providing government run "single payer" systems, the results have been discouraging, and once again, the Moderate Party wants people to learn from history. As part of the surge of State Socialism after WWII, and justified by the need for "a caring government", much of the health care systems in many countries were taken over by the government. But what emerged in country after country has been the growing realization that most of these government-based programs were serious failures. They have been characterized by a lack of even moderately good facilities; a shortage of medications and equipment, inexplicably low salaries for doctors and nurses and medical technicians, and an inability to adapt to new technologies. As a consequence, there has had to be a retreat from state provision to more private provision, and individual responsibility and choice. "People can't expect a free lunch". Yet there are influential interests in the U. S. who advocate exactly that. The Moderate Party would surely preserve the middle ground of a good deal of government involvement in a health care system in support of the truly needy that remains predominantly individual and private.

An emerging arena of policy contention is the debate about simplicity vs. complexity. We now have a population of more than 328 million people, this population is aging, and the range of illness and injury that can be dealt with has also expanded. Technology is indeed widening the ability of medicine to deal with a broader range of medical problems, and the consequence is that the whole system in all of its manifestations is becoming substantially more sophisticated and more expensive. There are expanding needs to deal with alcohol abuse, drug abuse, obesity, lack of knowledge, low threat control, better early warning and more penetrating diagnosis. An absolutely critical idea is the superiority of prevention rather than treatment, and this should be a major emphasis of the Moderate Party.

One extreme view being argued is that therefore, governments must take over health care because it is the only force that can adequately control it. But the prevailing view is that this attitude is seriously skewed, and that the health care system is in fact a sophisticated combination of more than 180 million insurance programs financed through employers; 166 million people covered by Medicare/Medicaid government programs; some 65 million people covered by health care savings plans; and special programs provided through the military establishment and the Veterans Administration.

But it is the almost universal view that far more serious efforts are needed to make the health care system simpler, cheaper, and more firmly anchored in private control. The Moderate Party would keep the reliance on individual responsibility, and having the bulk of health insurance provided by employers.

Complexity equals expense, and almost everyone agrees that the national system is too expensive. Why? First, drug manufacturer profit margins are suspected of being overinflated because of too little competition, too many monopoly situations, too little customer understanding of what costs really are, and too little political courage to regulate not drugs but profits. One justification centers around the costs of research and development. This is always cited by drug manufacturers as necessary predecessors to product development and it is in addition to the costs of drug manufacture and distribution. But it is also clear that this is an industry where there have been deliberate inflations of prices, and it is true that the whole system from manufacturing to insurance to medical care is hugely protected by high level special interest politics. The Moderate Party should go along with reasonable means to prevent excessive and unfair profits and system free loading. One of these unfair practices if the deliberate and ignorant belief that emergency care is somehow "free" and thus people do not need to buy expensive insurance – they just check in to the nearest hospital emergency service. But an option worth working out would be to charge emergency patients without health insurance, if they do have money. The fee for such care could be means tested. 6

What seems to be an excellent idea is for the creation of more "association health plans", available through small business and individual associations, featuring plans that are basic and cheap, excluding such things as previous illness, maternity costs, some prescription drugs, mental health care, etc.

This could be linked with a version of basic health insurance with limited duration. These ideas should be more vigorously linked to an emphasis on health care prevention; it is better and cheaper to prevent than to cure. One of the things that bother people is the fact they cannot, as individuals, figure out how to select the best doctor or hospitable. Some version of "Angies List" for evaluating doctors and hospitals might be a valuable approach to expand.

Then, there is the whole complex issue of abortion. There are powerful interests that have pursued forever a frenzied hyper partisan conflict, featuring two extremist alternatives — all yes or all no. Meanwhile, public opinion polls have constantly shown that at least 60% of the public favor a moderate position allowing abortion with certain legally defined limits, centered around human safety. 51% of the people polled favor pro-choice. 56% of those polled see it as morally wrong. The Moderate Party would favor a pro-choice policy, but with the limitations dealing with the wellbeing of the woman and fetus.

Above all is the overwhelming importance of employer provided insurance coverage. Of the total of 304 million insured people, 180 million are insured under an employer plan, 68 million are insured under Medicaid, and 55 million under Medicare. ACA insures only 11 million. Consider also the people insured by DOD and VA (where now 1/3 of patients are treated by private providers). In fact, there is very major satisfaction with the system alongside of the complaints, as for example polls that show that more than 80% of the elderly feel safe and adequately protected. The Moderate Party must choose, and ultimately would favor a reasonable expansion of Medicaid, the extension of parent policies, constant support of employer programs, an allotment system of funding to the states, subsidies for emergency treatment, but perhaps an increase in the eligibility age, at least for Medicare. Doctors and medical offices need the authority to deal directly with manufacturers and not through some middle man. In other words, upgrade the present system; do not attempt to destroy it.

An almost impossible problem is that of trying to deal with the costs of very expensive high-risk patients. Some drugs cost many thousands of dollars/ month. Recently the cost of one cancer medication was computed to be $16, 860 per month; another was computed at $18,670 per month. And another form of cost problem is the growing levels of opiate abuse, which has reached epidemic proportions in some places. It is a disturbing to believe that the new generation is inventing four new vices: legalized marijuana, a hugely increased range of poisonous opiates, electric cigarettes, and "vapping" whatever that is. It is particularly distressing to note that much of this problem lies with the actions of doctors, who over-prescribe, benefit from keeping their abuse "customers", and quietly support excessive opiate drug costs.

THE MODERATE PARTY AGENA

1. As always, the Party must be the supporter of an approach to health care that occupies a middle world of self-reliance, buttressed by government support, collaboration and moderation.
2. Every citizen should be covered by some form of health care protection unless he/she chooses not to be.
3. It is perfectly acceptable to have a health care system with has many forms and levels. It is not desirable to demand a single uniform and mandated system. There is great value in working toward programs that at simple, effective and less costly.
4. Instead of attempting to force businesses out of providing health insurance for their employees, the government should be actively helping businesses, especially small businesses to enhance the range and quality of care provided.
5. It will be desirable to be the sturdy backer of health care that promotes prevention over cure.
6. The Moderate Party should support and assist the provision of safe and feasible abortion care, but supported as much as possible by individual women or forms of private assistance.
7. If there are people who cannot be reached with health care now, it preferable to solve this lack by reasonable expansions of Medicare and Medicaid.
8. The Party must become a forceful and demanding means to attack the twin problems excessive greed and over-pricing throughout the health care world, and the disgraceful record in some arenas of rampant corruption.
9. The Party must expect to become the lead force in facing up to the growing national problems of drug addition and abuse.
10. People are normally not able to judge the qualifications of doctors, nurses and medical technicians. A valid idea would be the creation of some form of "Angies List" for the dispassionate rating of health care professionals.

EDUCATION: PRIMARY, UNIVERSITY AND BEYOND

First and foremost: The Moderate Party should recognize that elementary/ secondary education is a local government responsibility, best provided locally and directed by local interests including school boards, local governments and parents themselves. If there are inadequacies in some school program, it is surely the responsibility of local school boards and governments to solve the problems – not the Federal government. Most school systems are public rather than private, both is service delivery and management, and in policy determination and financing.

But there is some serious concern with the effectiveness of such systems. Concerns have become increasingly more compelling about the effectiveness of teaching and the relevance of course offerings to the demands of modern society. Part of this debate is the growing turmoil around broader social and political controversies over the racial or gender representation in classes, and the weakness of schools in predominantly black neighborhoods. It has also been argued that it is somehow "improper" to fail anybody, or the idea that students should not be prevented from graduation because of poor performance.

And emerging from these debates is the argument that private organizations would be freer, more versatile and more innovative than stagnant pubic organizations. And part of this suspicion of public schools is their critical failures in very poor neighborhoods, minority communities and urban ghettos. Then, seriously adding to this conflict is the fact that, in recent months, many public jurisdictions are increasingly facing the dilemma of inadequate financing, and 29 states have made substantial cuts E/S funding. More parents now feel that they want more and better education than public schools provide, and the growth of cities have led to the emergence of education through the private sector taking up the slack. Teachers unions which are staffed by public employees and are universally deep into Democrat Party politics and they have used their political clout to oppose private schools. Freedom from union power, more independent and effective school system management, and more attention to the needs of students instead of teachers should be the hallmark of Moderate Party policy.

It is also important to remember that there are very important sources of advanced education and training beyond universities. A very significant proportion of education and training take place in technical schools, vocational training provided by employers, formal On-The-Job (OJT) training programs, and enormous capacity and desire for people to learn skills on the job, and to promote their own self development.

In other words, "education" must be dealt with on this broader range. One of the key elements here is the question of whether formal education really provides the skills needed on the job, and this concern extends to teaching competence. Do teachers possess and teach the skills that allow young people to succeed in the actual real world? Not always. But the best answer to this question is to recognize the wide availability of privately based training capabilities very specifically linked to these needs.

Yet it is also true that the United States has produced the best college level system in the world: world class universities, high enrollments of foreign students, much of it government supported. In Germany, the university system is essentially free, with the government paying about $14,000 per student, plus another $3,000 in private or other funding. The comparable numbers in the U. S. is about $10,000 in public funding plus more than $20,000 in privately provided money for a total of over $30,000 per student. Much of that money ends up in university sponsored research, and our universities, for decades, have produced the highest level of research achievement in field after field. So it could be argued: "If it ain't broke, don't fix it!"

At the same time, there is increasing concern about what this system is costing both for schools and for governments and for students and their parents. Student debt is now about $1.4 trillion. More loans are being taken out, at higher and higher costs. Repayments have become a serious drag on students after graduation, and there is a growing debate over "the money shuffle" of who pays. It is argued thus, that the "answer" would be "free university education" provided by government. But surely it is obvious that such a system would not be "free" in any sane sense, and has it happened in other public programs, the access to government money might lead providers enthusiastically to raise their prices.

And then, there is the concerns about the universities themselves, as functioning institutions. Universities have become larger, more complex, and it is argued, more ponderous, confused and very much more costly, in some cases leading to increasing neglect of maintenance, repair, upgrading, and the ability to introduce new technologies. It is also a growing concern that they are falling into some new trap; on campuses, what should be "allowed" and what should be "prohibited." This has created not only great consternation within the schools, but in clashes with outside groups and interests. More education will be on line, but this obviously raises concerns about who will guarantee what is employed is correct, honest, proper and useful. Finally, there is the nasty perception that free tuition helps not the poorest of students but the richest.

THE MODERATE PARTY AGENDA

1. The Moderate Party should support the policy that elementary and secondary education should remain the primary responsibility of local governments, primarily cities, towns, and counties.
2. "If it ain't broke, don't fix it.
3. There is a need to expand the strength of the relationship between what is taught in universities and what is demanded in many kinds of jobs.
4. The Moderate Party must take on the enormous chore of broadly reducing the burdens of college debt, but this is not to be achieved by converting the entire university system to a "free" entirely government funded system.
5. In the process, universities themselves should become simpler, more understandable organizations, less ponderous and bureaucratic.

AGENDA NINE

SUCCESSFUL RETIREMENT

It may come as a big surprise to find out that, in the US, 80% of people over 65 say that they are financially secure.

But among the 50-65 age group, only 38% feel that they have been able to make adequate provision for retirement.

It is good public policy to aid those that cannot support themselves, but this should be based on the general philosophy that people must plan to provide for themselves. Now, ten thousand people a day reach 65, and this is a rising tide. But a large number of people, estimated as high as 48 million, have simply fumbled their preparation for retirement, and there is little sympathy for simply bailing them out. Yet the income figures from the Census Bureau are pretty encouraging. The U. S. median income is now about $61, 300. The poverty rate is defined as just 12.3%. The people without health care are only about 8.8%. But clearly, there is he is a critical need to somehow force more retirement planning and preparation. A big part of the problem is that many do not earn enough to put money away for retirement. Social security was never intended to be a full retirement provision, but as a supplement to self-provision, including reliance on the support of their children or relatives, which is reality in many countries. But mostly, there is a vexing preference to live it up today instead of the boring business of planning for "the future."

In the U. S., the importance of employer-based retirement systems is overwhelming. Also, the cost of retirement varies widely by location – e. g. New York vs. Wyoming. And increasingly, fears about retirement are driven by the seemingly endless increase in the high costs of health care, and of retirement homes. For many, the answer is to move the whole system to a "single payer" program, meaning funding by the government. This is seen as horribly expensive, and unnecessary for hundreds of millions of people who can will finance retirement by themselves. The counter concern is that the single payer government program will go the route of oppressive and bureaucratic government control, and the threat of endless corruption.

THE MODERATE PARTY AGENDA

1. The Moderate Party will have a relatively moderate role; it must continue to promote a current system that is meeting at least the basic retirement needs of most of our senior citizens.
2. It should reject the arguments for the conversion of the whole enormous population of elderly to some form of system entirely provided and controlled by the government.
3. Such a change would cut off large amounts of money now provided by retirees and their organizations, and unfortunately just shift the burden to the taxpayers.
4. It should become the zealot and advocate of urging people to make full and adequate planning for their own retirement.
5. Finally, we should manage to avoid the creation of an enormous government bureaucracy.

TRANSPORTATION AND INFRASTRUCTURE

Another utterly fascinating tax battlefield centers around the question of which level of government gets to collect what taxes and for what purpose. In one direction, there are many public programs which are shared between governments at several levels. Others may be mandated by federal law but with performance solely at the local level. In other cases, local government politicians and managers think it would be a good idea to get the federal government to pick up at least part of the cost of any number of programs.

An example is that of the great national network of highways, roads and streets, and of the vehicles that run over them. The U. S. government has, over the last 60 years, developed this vital network of interstate highways, knitting the country together as never before. This network is supplemented by additional roads that are state owned and operated, but partially funded by the federal government because they are designed to link the interstate system with local roads. Then, as in every state, there is a system of highways and roads strictly to meet state demands, and these are state funded, and this network can be of critical value to rural and small town areas where there are long distances between remote homes and scarce public facilities such as schools and hospitals. Finallly, small towns and big metropolitican areas alike all need extensive and often very complicated nets of streets. And after we count the 250 million private cars — start thinking about the 130 million trucks!

The whole complex pattern of highway infrastructure is endlessly repeated in the world of airports, airlines, traffic control and safety regulation. It is almost inconceivable to recognize that there are now 59 million air passengers per year, and another source threatens "246 million passengers this summer"! Then explain how to deal with ships, cargo, trains and rails and stations, ports, and huge complex terminals for handling freight.

Paying for this huge and complex system features three eternal struggles. First is the need to obtain the funds to build this infrastructure in the first place. Second is the infighting over which level of government pays for what. Third is the ominous and increasing concern about the deterioration and decline of these roads, streets and bridges, and the need to come up with a whole new funding strategy for "maintenance and repair". The inexorable incease in national population and the vast increase in the number of cars and trucks on the road, and the number of destinations has overtaken existing capabilities. From the federal level, the political preference is that the feds finance only the interstate system and closely related state roads. Local officials seem to want two things: avoidance of demands for state delivery of more capability without accompanying funding (the dreaded "unfunded mandate"), but perversely, stout lobbying in Washington to solicit federal funding even for infrastructure responsibilities that are clearly the responsibilities of the state. While federal funds have increased by 7% in recent years, this has just barely kept up with inflation, but in the meantime, 30 states have in fact raised their gas taxes mostly by the politically simpler approach of linking the tax rate to the general index.

This transportation example illustrates the utter complexity of intergovernmental financing across practically the whole spectrum of American public programs. Even the military establishment, which is clearly a national government responsibility still, in some cases, imposes cost burdens on local governments. The Moderate Party would have to establish some sensible control of the tendency for overregulation of this sector – its excessive planning, the burden of the public review and comment regulations, the legal mandates, the overlap of federal, state, county and city regulations, the hundreds of agencies, boards, commissions, task forces, on and on. Then there is the ominous unwillingness to face up to the sector's financial fears and shortcomings. In other words, the prevalence of bad bureauracy must be faced. The grip of special interest politics is particularly strong in this sector, and there a tendency to overstate problems hoping to extrude more money. Urban interests are particularly scared because they are the most at risk.

THE MODERATE PARTY AGENDA

1. Problem number one is the financing of new infrastructure. In the past, there has been a more or less clear separation between what is federal and what is local, and what is primarily the responsibility of private sector interests. The tendency now it to see these interests blend together, and the new imperative is to produce a national system for infrastructure that is far more collaborative and cooperative.

2. Problem number two is the willingness of political leaders and program managers to face up to the growing need for maintenance and repair. This has become a classic case of political cowardice, but reality is descending rapidly, and hard decisions are forcing themselves forward.

3. Problem number three is the question of 'who pays", but increasingly, the answer is "everybody" and the job of the party will be to get the leadership to face up to reality.

4. One of the collateral problems is that, over time, the urge to regulate all of the forms of transportation and public infrastructure systems excessively, harming these services and raising their costs. It would be the role of the Party to make a major effort to curb this pattern of overregulation.

5. In a similar vein, the government bureaucracies involved are massively duplicative and bureaucratic, and urgently need to be thinned out and simplified.

IMMIGRATION AND REFUGEES

The whole issue of the great surge of enforced movement of people is clouded by the fact that there are so many complex reasons for such movement. What is quite normal in the United States and most other countries is that there are always very large numbers of people with legitimate reasons to leave their existing living places and seek opportunities somewhere else. The United States has a long and marvelous history of acceptance of immigrants from all over the world. In this process, there is insistence that, in order to be allowed in, the immigrants must show some capacity to take care of themselves, including worker skills, or the support of American persons or organizations. Part of the concern is the question of immigrants can do when they get in. There is the fear that immigrants "steal" jobs from current people; but the most recent perception is the old one: America produces lots of jobs, and somehow immigrants search them out.

There needs to be a distinction drawn between immigrants and refugees. In the United States we have about 43 million immigrants both legal and illegal, with the legal entry level capped at 140,000 per year. Refugees are defined as people who are forced to flee their homes by some form of attack, even by some foreign government, and there are now at least 25 million refugees at float in the world. The law demands that their desire to enter is driven by the established fact that they have been oppressed and forced to flee, and that they cannot return to their homes for fear of persecution. But this is often almost impossible to prove, beyond what the individuals say. There is a fear that there are now so many refugees from so many sources that the US could be overwhelmed, as Europe now feels. The normal desire to aid the oppressed is counterbalanced by the enormous costs that can be demanded, and the feeling that, somehow, we have been duped.

With respect to immigrants, there is a widely held fear that many immigrants are bad guys – MS-13, crooks, dead-beats, free loaders, drug smugglers, gun runners, thieves, murderers, rapists, etc. Thus, most people favor border control in some form, but appear to doubt that "the "Wall" will really be adequate. We must resist the almost hysterical fear of the hoard of people who might storm our borders: consider the size of the populations of major losing countries: Honduras, 9 million; El Salvador, 6 million; Haiti, 10 million; Nicaragua, 6 million, Costa Rico, 5 million, for a total of 36 million. But also consider: Mexico, 122 million, Cuba, 11 million, Venezuela, 29 million; Colombia, 47 million, Panama, 4 million, for a total of 213 million. Thus, in the "worst case", there is a pool of 249 million people living under oppressive governments, and thus are possible immigrant or refugee candidates.

So we need a policy that lets in the good guys, keep out the bad guys, and keeps the total influx down to manageable levels. Keeping out the bad guys warrants an effective border control system: not just a "Wall" but a coherent border management system including a competent and supported staff of professional control officers, vehicles, aircraft, communications and even weapons. 64% of the American population sees this as one of the most serious problems facing the country, but they also overwhelmingly oppose the separation of families, and curse the "stupid" government. The Moderate Party policy: recognize that the great majority of both immigrants and refugees will be decent human beings, wanting good and normal lives. Provide a secure path for achievement of citizenship.

The federal government has blotted its own record by failing to treat all immigrants and refugees humanely. Part of the problem clearly is lack of money. (although a $4.6 billion aid bill has just been enacted). Part of the problem is that everybody along the Mexican border is simply overwhelmed, including the Mexicans themselves. Part of the problem is politicians are so busy scoring points against each other that they have no time to legislate solutions. Blanket and uncontrolled "decriminalization" is not a valid solution. It is unsatisfactory to realize that there are more than 900,000 people already in the country who are waiting for their review in one of the special immigrant courts. Perhaps the Moderate Party would finally have the courage to solve the money problem, and then hire a major hotel chain to provide adequate housing and services under contract to a smarter government overseer.

But such a policy should include what is ominous and very unpopular. It is to propose that more people living under oppressive regimes should stay home and fight it out. The people of more than forty countries around the world are doing just that, and we can point to the fact that the people of Sudan have recently overthrown one of the worst dictators in the world.

THE MODERATE PARTY AGENDA

1. The basic policy is just to treat all people, whether immigrants or refugees as decent human beings, and all policies should be centered around this perception.
2. The problems of dealing with immigrants and refugees are capable of being handled. There are no "missions impossible" confronting the government or indeed the people. The problems will be vexing, and the consequences will be expensive, but they can and should be handled.
3. But it is legitimate to work to stem the flow of potential incoming people, and it is fair to undertake measures to do so. There should never be an "open border" philosophy.
4. The Party should face up to advocating a troubling an unpopular position that there must be people around the world that must simply stand and fight.
5. For those who enter, all must find a real path to citizenship, and a government that will help them along that path and not be the source of obstruction.
6. Still – it is perfectly acceptable for both governments and citizens to work hard to keep out the "bad buys".

FAIR AND ADQUATE TAXATION

The American system of taxes has not kept up with the tides running in the economy, and society in general. Our world is increasingly urban, middle class and consumer driven. It is centered around its industrial past and the old traditional skills of farming, fishing, forestry, mining, transportation, but manufacturing has gradually been overtaken by its own success because it created and financed the surge of the consumer economy that dominates today. Our economic world is driven by banking and finance, communications, higher education, government, and millions of jobs in offices, retail establishments and service organizations. Picks and shovels have been replaced by the computer. Massive shifts have occurred fromt the rural village to urban life – the life of the future. The financial fear is very real. We are already experiencing massive deficits in government budgets at all levels – 78% of GDP now as opposed to 37% on 1991. And Democrat Party candidates for president are almost all advocating monstrous, gigantic new public programs like free"Medicare for All", free college education, free child care, teacher pay subsidies, elimination of current college debt, and consequences of extensive social changes such as a higher minimum wage, guaranteed gender wages, and the undefined and incomprehensible "Green New Deal'.

Some forms of taxation have special importance in the overall system. Consider the following:

1. No tax

It is important and gratifying to remember that the U. S. tax system allows some 42% of low income people to pay no federal income tax at all – the world's greatest tax relief system! But increasingly, everybody – companies, rich people, poor people, middle class people – resents taxes even if employed for "noble" purposes, and taxes almost always seen as "too high" or "too low". Thus, there is a growing concern that the tax system is somehow obsolete; that it needs to be streamlined and simplified and modernized; and that it's sense of priority needs to be more at <u>ME</u> and not at <u>THEM.</u>

Further, there is the sense that the whole system is perverted; that there are too many loopholes, special interest advantages, and trap doors and escape hatches for the crafty and the greedy and the illegals to step through. People are outraged when they see "their money" misdirected, and nobody seems to care.

2. The fuel tax

For more than 60 years, both federal a local governments have imposed a special tax on the sale of auto fuel, with the funds credited to a special trust fund to finance the national highway system and related state or urban roads, streets and mass transit. This can claim to be one of the most successful tax programs in modern government history because it has led to the creation of a network that has tied the country together. But the national population has greatly increased, the number of trucks and autos has skyrocketed, the roadways are showing increasing wear, and there is now an obvious need either to increase the amount of this tax, or to find other sources of revenue. The fear now is that the political leadership at all government levels lacks the will or the courage to bite this bullet.

3. The Social Security tax

This tax was created in 1935 as a valuable response to the plight of the elderly in a Depression driven economy. It was clear from the start that income from Social Security payouts was never intended as a full funding of individual retirement costs, but was to be a supplement and safety net added to the funds saved by each individual.

Over the years, the government have struggled to deal with the demands of a far larger population of retirees, with the inflation in the economy, the rising costs of living, and with a populist political tendency to buy popularity with public money by increasing payment levels. In the end, this tax is treated as sacred, and somehow it retains its high human value.

4. Medicare taxes

Mainly, this is a tax on employment income, since the great majority of health insurance is provided in connection with employment. Each employee is required to pay 1.45% of wages and salaries as a tax, and the employer is required to match this with a matching 1.45%. In addition, in 2013, an additional surtax of .9% was levied on employee wages and salaries. Self employed persons must pay both of these taxes, or a total of 2.9%. Huge amounts of money are involved, but the rising costs of health care, and the shifts of a large cadre of people from employment to retirement seems to threaten the stability and adequacy of this system.

5. Import/Export taxes

It is probably true that these taxes are less important as revenue producers than they are as tools to manipulate economic activity. Import taxes are widely used by governments around the world to fend off foreign goods or services that compete with domestic producers. In many state socialist countries a policy of Import Substitution initiatives (ISI) became a crucial element of economic policy.

There are two moderate versions of ISI policy – a "domestic content" policy and a "mandated exporting" policy. In many countries, foreign direct investment (FDI) was deliberately limited. Whole sectors of a national economy were not open for foreign investment, and in most cases, foreign investment was limited to minority holdings of local enterprises to force foreign investors to partner with domestic enterprises and use locally produced raw materials, fabricated parts or subassemblies, and domestic labor. This policy is almost purely political and is widely used; it is even popular in the U. S., as witnessed by Buy American policies enacted into some laws and regulations, and the recent embargo policies of the Trump Administration.

All of these centrist government policies proved to have value only in the short run and only in cases where a country private sector was very weak. But all proved to be pathological in the longer term. Import substitution had the effect of depriving national consumers of superior foreign products in favor of what all too often proved to be inferior local products. Domestic content regulations were almost always quickly abandoned simply because they seriously inhibited the willingness of foreign investors to invest in a country where the government officially forced them to combine with obsolete or inefficient local enterprises

The economy of America has shifted radically away from earlier simpler forms to an economy that is more service/consumer based, and the national education system is sufficiently extensive and capable to meet new talent demands. Failure to do this would reduce the potential for more profitable and value added investments in the future. One of the biggest concerns expressed for example about the influx of illegal immigrants into the U. S. is that most of these people are underskilled and are fit only to hold the kinds of jobs that no longer exist in sufficient numbers. Yet there are many arenas of the economy that are searching for employees, and the immigrant/refugee population may be a valuable worker source after all.

7. The Value Added Tax (VAT)

Another form of taxation widely being debated is the Value Added Tax (VAT). This tax is essentially a tax on consumption rather than income, and it has been widely adopted in other countries. It is seen as a replacement for the income tax, or at least a supplement to a substantially reduced income tax system. It is argued that such a tax would be far easier to collect since it would be "built in" to the money collection systems of producers, and not in the form of complex income tax paperwork prepared by millions of confused and unhappy individuals. At the same time, there are two major objections to such a tax. First and foremost, it is regressive; it impacts most on individuals at the lower levels of income. A poor person and a billionaire pay the same tax. Then, companies protest, because they fear that the VAT is an expense that would have to be recovered either by higher prices for their customers, or by lower profits for its managers and stockholders. Finally, state or local governments that have already imposed sales taxes on consumer products and much else, fear that these local taxes would be driven out by an overbearing federal tax imposition.

8. The Carbon Tax

Another and very recent new tax proposal would be the imposition of a carbon tax, which would be levied against any source of energy that adds carbon to the atmosphere. Here, the objective is clearly the enforcement of a government policy and not primarily the raising of revenue. Its advocates argue that this is a "win-win" idea – the environment is protected and government gets rich. The counter argument of course is that the burden of an added tax (level not yet defined) would, in the short run, simply get passed off to the users of the energy source, and in the long run, would inhibit the development of manufacturing and energy supply to cope with future national population expansion, and new and more demanding technologies. Part of this counter argument is that new technology will also include the development of new and more effective means to reduce carbon emissions, and this would be a "positive" solution as opposed to a tax "negative". Additional debates are simmering at a lower level about new taxes of a punitive nature such as a tax on marijuana sales or even on soft drinks with high sugar content, but public resistance to these ideas have a new tone where the public doubts that such taxes would really cut usage, and they are increasingly resented as government oppression and arrogance, and about the desire of governments to meddle endlessly in people;s lives.

At a second level below the broad role of defining what taxes to impose is another set of issues dealing with how the tax system is really administered. At this level, a whole new array of gaming and manipulation is in play. The laws and regulations define and elaborate hundreds of different taxes – arcane, complex, legalistic, deliberately or inadvertantly obscure, wholly inexplicable, controversial, contradictory, often outrageous and often obsolete. This is the chosen playground of countless politicians, corporate executives, foundation directors and a vast army of tax lawyers happily and profitably harvesting the benefits of this field of governance. Here are some of the sub plots that the tax system offers.

9. Tax expenditures

This is a tool for goverance at it's most patronizing. "Expenditure" really means "taxes we could have collected, but we are generous and we won't". Thus, the government acts as if it had collected the tax but had then given it back. The classic example is that the government does not collect a tax on home mortgages paid by people, and this particular sophistry has been going on for more than 70 years. The U. S. Department of the Treasury defines it as "revenue losses attributable to provisions of the Federal tax laws which allow a special exclusion, exemption, or deduction from gross income or which provide a special credit, a preferential rate of tax, or a deferral of tax liability." Given this latitude, tax expenditures may be used as an alternative to other government policy instruments such as spending within the Federal budget, or some form or regulatory relief. The largest tax expenditures are exclusion of employer contributions for medical insurance premiums and medical care. ($2.74 billion); exclusion of net imputed rental income ($1.0 billion); capital gains, except for agriculture, timber, iron ore, coal ($1.0 billion); and deductability of mortgage interest on owner-occupied homes ($948 million). In addition, the federal government supports the system of mortgage financing. The Federal National Mortgage Association ('Fanny Mae"), and the Federal Home Loan Mortgage Corporation ("Freddie Mac") both bundle mortages into long term securities. Both are owned by shareholders and are profit-making, but both collapsed during the financial crisis of 2008, and as a consequence, the government wants to make GNMA a direct guarantor of mortgage backed securities as a future crisis prevention measure.

10. Tax waivers

Waivers are often sophisticated maneuvers; a game any number can play, and it seems that almost everyone does. In a sense, this is the most interesting, but also the most disturbing feature of the entire utterly confusing tax system. In essence, Congress will pass a law enabling the collection of some form of tax, but the same law may permit some often undefined latitude in how the tax is collected. In some cases, the tax may be waived or simply not collected. In other cases, only a reduced percentage of the tax is collected and the rest is foregone. Or the government may assert that the tax can be collected, but then the payer is somehow exempted. In some unpopular cases, taxes may be imposed where not otherwise applicable, as a form of government punishment.

It doesn't take much imagination to recognize that this is a fertile field for sophisticated maneuver. This is the home for the skilled manipulator. Every corporation, foundation, association or individual – or crook – seems to have set out to obtain some form of this advantage. The District of Columbia and environs is simply full of lobbyists, lawyers, representatives, and friends of the politicians and agency officials, working all the angles and pressing all the buttons. This is the very home and target and playground for our national problem of the primacy of special interest politics. At the second, or third, or fifth level of hundreds of laws and regulations there are thousands of little obscure, arcane paragraphs and sentences which open up the trap door of some tax collection machine. Often, these maneuvers represent bribes offered and taken. But most of the time, theft is not necessary, and craft and guile are sufficient. If there is a legitimate and compelling need for "tax reform" this is surely the place.

11. Corporate taxes

Corporations in America are the strength and the life blood of our economy, and they range from huge international conglomerates, down to corner hot dog stands. In theory, almost nobody agrees that these companies should not have to pay taxes, so the real arguments center around what they pay for and how much. These arguments in turn butt up against two additional debates of absolutely crucial importance. The first argument suggests that it is probable that a corporation paying a tax will simply fold this cost into the prices it charges its customers, or as back pressure against what it must pay to suppliers, or the wages and benefits it must supply to its employees. If customers and suppliers can successfully resist corporate pressure, this will be argued back against the government imposition of taxes in the first place.

The second momentous argument is that corporations are the key to national economic development – that the economy will not grow and innovate and produce greater national wealth unless corporations lead the charge. It follows then, it is asserted, that if government taxes are too stringent, this would inhibit the desire and the ability of the private sector to enhance the economy. This in turn will have the effect of reducing the profits that the government taxes to generate its own revenues

An example is that of the great national network of highways, roads and streets, and of the vehicles that run over them. The U. S. government has, over the last 60 years, developed this vital network of interstate highways, knitting the country together as never before. This network is supplemented by additional roads that are state owned and operated, but partially funded by the federal government because they are designed to link the interstate system with local roads. Then, as in every state, there is a system of highways and roads strictly to meet state demands, and these are state funded, and this network can be of critical value to rural and small town areas where there are long distances between remote homes and scarce public facilities such as schools and hospitals. Finallly, small towns and big metropolitican areas alike all need extensive and often very complicated nets of streets. But the ultimate fact is that this complex and often contentious system usually works.

12. The Wealth Tax; There is now a surging political proposal to condemn what is seen as the ominous and immoral accumulation of excess wealth by the very richest people and institutions in the U. S., and it is further argued that when the rich are more deeply taxed, the government income could then totally finance the whole range of new or expanded public programs. Thus, the expansion of populist political promises could magically be financed without having to raise the taxes of the middle classes.

THE MODERATE PARTY AGENDA

1. **First of all, the need for total system reform**. The Party must recognize that it must reverse the fact that gaming and preferment are more powerful than the courage to reform. Because of this, the whole system is viewed by the public and some of the political leadership with dark suspicion, and reform could take advantge of this public support. The general perception now is that the system is "arcane, far too complex, confusing, incomprehenible, legalistic, contradictory, and often obsolete".

2. The ultimate first step to such reform would be to enact laws that **tighten controls on borrowing, and set upper limits on indebtedness.**

3. **Tax subsidies.** Eliminate some substantial number of preferential subsidies now carefully embedded in the system in exchange for a general reduction in the level of taxation of corporate income. Above all, the Party should vigorously resist government imposed import substitution taxes.

4. **Spending reduction.** The ultimate influence on the tax system is to the reduce the demand for taxation by reducing government expenditures. While strictly not tax reform almost every tax reform study has emphasized this point.

5. **Tax evasion.** Reform would have three components. First, the system itself can be improved in ways that eliminate gaps and loopholes that are openings for tax evasion. Second, the system could be made to provide more serious penalties for tax evasion. Third, pursuit of tax evaders can be made more vigorous and successful.

6. **Fraudulent refunds.** The Government Accountability Office (GAO), an agency supporting the Congress has urged the federal

government to prevent paying hundreds of millions of dollars in fraudulent refunds year after year after year.

7. **Special interest purge.** Mount a major assault on special interest advantages: a purging of the whole tax code of special interest breaks and tax loopholes, especially for profit making organizations.

8. **Tax collection:** The government needs to be much more serious about collecting all taxes due – on time. Strengthen the ability to collect taxes.

    Enact legislation to reform overly suppressive **tort laws.**

9. **Reduce tax expenditures.** One of the most politically popular forms of tax evasion is the deliberate public policy of deciding not to collect certain taxes that might have been collected. An example is a tax on payment of home mortages which are forgone for most home owners.

10. **Eliminate estate "death" taxes.** One of the most powerful of such tax expenditure targets is any tax on the estates of people when then die. It is argued that assets of an estate have already been taxed when they were earned, and that it is unfair to tax them again.

11. **Greater public knowledge.** Legislative bodies or offices of a President should be required to publish a list of all tax advantages contained in the tax code, and their costs. Tax laws are also prime targets for limited time authorizations.

12. **Expand the tax base** to all but the very poor. More than 40% of American earners pay no federal taxes, but many often very profitable companies also pay little or no taxes through legal and regulatory maneuvering. There should be no policy to subsidize profit making businesses, and every business should be made to pay its "fair share".

13. **But – corporate size.** A good case can be made for more carefully designing the tax structure so that, in a common sense way, it puts a greater burden on large and wealthy businesses, and is kinder and lighter on small business owners. There is a genuine argument about the immorality of mammoth corporations.

14. **The special case of health care.** There is increasing concern about the soaring costs of health care, and it is felt that significant savings could be realized if these costs can be controlled. This might involve reform of Medicare payments to doctors and health workers, and by placing firm limits on potential future cost increases. There is no compelling case to dislodge the whole national health care system by enacting 'Medicare For All" and many more moderate reforms are

feasible. Perhaps the most serious kind of proposal for both Medicare and Medicaid is to retrench the range of program eligibility, by a means test or an age test.

15. **Other spending reforms.** Similar arguments are advanced for other federal programs such as Social Security; the Supplemental Nutritional Assistance Program (SNAP, earlier called the Food Stamp Program), farm subsidies, local school aid, and more.

16. **A gas tax.** This highly successful tax has not kept up with inflation, and it is more than time to upgrade it. Deterioration of streets and highways is becoming a more serious problem, and the possibilities of other forms of funding for this infrastructure range from slim to none. Here is the perfect issue where the Moderate Party would need to stand up and be counted.

17. One highly regarded option, widely used in Europe and elsewhere is what is known as a **value added tax**. The argument here is that the VAT is probably not regressive, and it is a better and simpler and less expensive form of tax collection. Local governments fear that such a consumer based tax will clash with their own efforts to impose local government sales taxes. The Moderate Party should accept this reasoning and avoid a substantial new tax imposed on consumers.

18. The **wealth tax.** The Moderate Party would accept that the distribution of national wealth has indeed shifted too far in favor of the very rich, and it is fair to adjust the tax structure to indeed tax the rich. There would be two exceptions. First, we should avoid taxing the increases in wealth and assets resulting from SUCCESS – from skill and entrpreunrship, and initiative. Second, we should avoid the mistake of tax changes that, either deliberately or inadvertantly, reward the rich, as for example, the idea of free college education that ends up predomonintly rewarding the children of the rich, or government health insurance plans that give free medical care to billionaires. The increase in wealth from the successes of the economy such as inheritance taxes or increases in land value can legitimately be taxed.

MODERATING THE URGE TO REGULATE

The essence of regulation is to require people and institutions to change the way they act and think, and for most of the time, there was the general perception that regulation by the government was very important by preventing abuses in the economy and society. But increasingly, the broadening span of government programs and the growing sophistication of American society has led to an extremely broad increase in the magnitude and impact of government regulation. This in turn is forcing the question: when is government regulation warranted, and when does it go beyond reason and become an instrument of oppression? One of the risks associated with government regulation is that the regulated industries learn to "play the game" better than their government supervisors, and in effect, capture the regulatory apparatus, by fair means or foul. Then, regulations can be softened or avoided, enforcement can be fended off, oversight can be made friendlier, and price or cost control regulations mysteriously turned to the advantage of the regulated.

But most of the time, the power of the government is so strong that a pathological regime can easily use regulation as a form of tyranny designed deliberately to enhance the power of an authoritarian regime, and provide the basis for reward of one's friends and punishment of one's enemies. It must constantly be remembered that the old Socialist promise to support people "from the cradle to the grave", really turned out to mean controlling people from the cradle to the grave. It has also proved all too possible to avoid the consequences of regulations that would quash corruption such as prohibitions against bribery, influence peddling, money laundering, concealment of assets, extortion, malfeasance, misfeasance, and others.

Regulations are tough to deal with because they are so complicated and technical. At best, this can be mitigated by careful public education and explanation. At worst, public ignorance is deliberate and highly prized by the holders of power, the happy home of thousands of special interests. Governments can select from an almost unlimited variety of tools in the regulatory tool kit: price regulation, import/export limitations; quotas, tariffs; granting or withholding of licenses and permits; health and safety regulations for every segment of the economy; franchising and licensing; controls for anti-trust, anti-monopoly and anti-cartel mechanisms; and control of the right to do business. Regulations are limitless in their scope, obscure in their technical detail, open to extrapolation and interpretation, and selective in their application.

Overregulation is common, and it can be deliberate and political. Politicians find it easier to write broad regulatory authority; it gives them endless opportunities to control a power base that makes everybody else pleaders for something. Overregulation simply gives officials more points of leverage to broker their own power, creating the basis for "selective" regulation where officials can choose what to enforce and how, and in the process, regulators can become petty, tyrannical, mean spirited and, especially, corrupt. If policy is the arena of the big tyrant, regulation is the arena of the petty tyrant.

Even in moderate and respected governments, enforcement can be a very corrosive role since it is used to make people or institutions do things that they may not want to do, and the more intrusive the regulations, the more likely it is that they will be resisted by both people and institutions. Ultimately, excessive regulation can breed suspicion of government itself. Political ambition or an excess of regulatory zeal may produce regulations that are managerial "missions impossible" – dreams or hopes of perfection rather than rules that are capable of being achieved. In countries with multiple layers of government such as the U. S., there are serious problems of duplication and even conflict of regulatory power and authority, and overpowering examples of the tyranny of intensely bureaucratic enforcement of the power to regulate.

In this regard, it is worth while to repeat in detail a damning commentary from George Will, reported in the Washington Post on June 25, 2017: "It took nine years just for permitting of a San Diego desalination plant. Five years and 20,000 pages of environmental assessments and permitting and regulatory materials were consumed before beginning to raise the roadway on New Jersey's Bayonne Bridge, as project which had virtually no environmental impact (it uses existing foundations and "rights of way"). Fourteen years were devoted to the Port of Savannah, which has been an ongoing process for almost 30 years. While faux environmentalists ligitate against modernizing of the U. S. electrical grid, transmission lines waste 6 percent of the electricity they transmit, which is equal to the output of 200 average size coal burning power plants. In 2011, shippers using inland waterway systems of canals, dams, and locks still endured delays amounting to 25 years. In 2012, the Treasury Department estimated that traffic congestion wasted 1.9 billion gallons of gasoline annually. Analysis shows that a six year delay in starting construction of public projects costs the nation over $3.7 trillion. America could modernize its infrastructure at half the cost, while dramatically enhancing environmental benefits, with a two year approval process."

There are not any agreed upon definitions or even intellectual limits on the theoretical power of governments to regulate, and there is a tendency of regulators to expand and extrapolate the range and depth of their regulations. Abuses of regulatory power have created a growing feeling that governments can and do go too far, and there are no effective means to limit the expansion of such power. Regulation is intensely bureaucratic: complicated, technical hard to understand, and often lacking adequate justification for their creation. Enforcement is usually costly and time consuming, requiring long time delays, and excessive paperwork. And regulations, once imposed can prove to be highly rigid, difficult to change, protected by their special interest backers, and almost immortal.

Regulation tends to become an end in itself. There is such a thing as "the regulatory mind" where the tendency is to believe that each body of regulation is vital, and thus needs to be broadened and deepened; to be extrapolated in application; and to be pushed down into second and third levels of detail. Many oppressive regulations are unwarranted extrapolations of a basically sound statute. Regulations may be a form of legislative abdication or at least shifting of some of the legislative role to the agency regulators — because legislative bodies did not have the front-end understanding of the whole consequence of the creation of a regulatory policy, nor the technical expertise to legislate specifics. But according to Philip K. Howard in his book "The Rule of Nobody", "The law (for regulation) is seen as a tool for self-interest, not as a beacon of fairness. The first flaw of the cherished philosophy of moral neutrality is that neutrality is impossible." We have unfortunately lost much of the acceptance of self-regulation, both individuals and organizations. Think of the problems of really trying to control any elements of a people population which now exceeds 328 million.

Why do Governments regulate? There are, of course many legitimate reasons. Some such as the following are for economic policy reasons (Bingman, "Why Governments Go Wrong"):

1. To promote economic "efficiency": i.e. to preserve market competition, to prevent excess profits, or to promote fair prices for value received.
2. To induce competition in any given market.
3. To control entry into a market place: controlling the issuance of licenses to do business; setting minimum standards of business or individual professional performance.
4. To require disclosure of economic information such as ownership, financial assets, level of debt, or legal challenges.
5. To prevent unacceptable public risks: examples include information about stock issues or financial risks (e.g. the savings and loan disaster).
6. To provide national uniformity of certain ground rules (e.g. conflicts of regulatory authority between the federal government and the states).
7. To limit competition in certain sectors (i.e. public utilities, maritime transport)
8. To redistribute income (i.e. minimum wage, labor protection)
9. To allocate scarce resources (e.g. Federal Communications Commission allocation of broadcast rights; access to natural resources on public lands).
10. To control economic outcomes (e.g. banking stability; home mortgage security; performance standards; anti-trust controls, etc.).

Other regulations are for social policy reasons:

1. To provide national or specific standards to assure equity, fairness and equality in issues of race, gender, ethnicity, cultural beliefs.
2. To preserve and enforce public/private rights (i.e. voting, civil rights, health and safety protections).

3. To prevent injustice (e.g. cheating, misrepresentation, failure to perform under contracts, freedom from civic or government abuse of authority, etc.).

4. To prevent or control anti-social behavior (e.g. sexual harassment).

5. To redistribute public power and prevent the abuse of power (requirements for public participation in government decisions; appeals against government actions, etc.).

In examining this listing of the legitimate purposes of regulation, it is unsettling but illuminating to recognize how each power can be perverted and made either pathological or corrupt or both. Regulation has become one of the most powerful tools by which governments enforce their will, and in countless countries around the world, regulations are in fact powerful tools for oppression. The power to regulate can be given to almost every government agency at all levels, and it is used to redirect institutional and individual behavior by defining what is prohibited and what is "allowed". The proliferation of regulations is so great in some countries, nobody including those who write them and enforce them understands them all, much less understanding their consequences, which can be enormous.

Almost nothing in society and life is unregulated, and nobody can say when it should stop and at what level. The Federal Register is now approaching 100,000 pages. The Code of Federal Regulations now has 41 volumes, plus 242 volumes of detailed regulations totaling more than 178,000 pages. Regulations are now not only far more numerous, but they are longer, much more complex, more detailed and far more difficult to prepare and gain approval.

The basic questions remain the hardest to answer. How safe is safe? How safe is safe enough? What, in society, should be left essentially unregulated? When and why does regulation become excessive and pathological? For the regulatory mind, the answer seems to be Never!

Another hard question is how far the imperatives of governance and the need to execute public policy should be permitted to overpower the rights of individuals and of institutions. Most people favor control of private sector institutions, at least with respect to public health and safety, but are often not aware of the many powerful but subtle means by which their own individual rights are also constrained.

Governments have proved universally and notoriously unable to regulate themselves. Laws intended to protect the public are often drawn too broadly and given too much room for perverse interpretation and the abuse of power. Political leaders can and do violate even well-defined regulations. Many regulations contain the power to allocate valuable resources, and this has proved to be an enormous source of corruption.

Further, each regulatory authority defined in some enabling statute has precipitated enormous volumes of second and third level regulations generated by the responsible regulatory agency, so voluminous and complicated that nobody can understand them all, even the people who enforce them. Then, bureaucrats may play the game of "selective" application of which regulations they choose to enforce, and which they might be motivated to ignore. Most regulations are highly technical and complex, and it very difficult to find a basis for challenging those that are seen as unnecessary or perverse. This is the major source of power for the government interpreters of these regulations, and of potential corruption in governments.

Problems of Regulatory Enforcement

Ultimately, excessive regulation can breed suspicion of government itself. Political ambition or an excess of regulatory zeal may produce regulations that are managerial "missions impossible" – dreams or hopes of perfection rather than practical rules that are capable of being achieved. In the United States with its complex multiple layers of government there are serious problems of duplication and even conflict of regulatory power and authority, and overpowering examples of the tyranny of intensely bureaucratic enforcement of the power to regulate.

The counter reaction to excessive regulation has led to a new interest in what effective alternatives to regulation could be used, and the Moderate Party should base its policies and actions on developing such options, along with a major policy position based on two themes: first, to act always to reduce government regulatory overburden, and second, to try to aim government regulation as much as possible toward a policy of facilitation enablement and assistance, as opposed to prohibition, limitation and opposition. Some specific policies would include the following:

1. We should want deliberately to decide more carefully that there should be some functions in society that need not be regulated (religion? personal privacy?). The basic question is whether there

are elements of society that can be trusted to conduct their activities with only general community oversight and not official government regulatory oversight.

2. The public can be protected by public education instead of, or in partial implementation by hastening toward official limitation and control. Voluntary controls are feasible in many areas and should be tried before government application of controls. Most corporations exercise voluntary use of independent auditors to provide public assurance of legality and probity as a vital element of business conduct.

3. Professional standards are a widely used and highly effective means of assuring publicly acceptable outcomes. Doctors are strongly motivated to observe professional ethics in the treatment of patients. Professional engineers are motivated to build bridges or dams that will not collapse. Teachers and university professors usually want to teach the truth. Professional managers have personal reputations at stake, and in many cases, managerial experience and judgment are superior to hard regulatory mandates. In their book "Public Policymaking by Private Organizations", Fritschler, Rudder, Choi), they state "private groups such as the American Bar Association, or Underwriters Laboratories, or the National Association of Home Builders, make and enforce rules that function like government's laws and regulations, and that this service has proved highly successful."

Instruments other than regulation may be employed. The tax system can be used to design rewards or penalties to achieve acceptable outcomes in lieu of regulation. There may also be rewards/penalties available through fiscal allocation.

Regulatory statutes when enacted are usually followed by a "lock-in" of clientele interests, and regulatory statutes are enormously difficult to change especially if change involves a shift in power. Thus, a regulation may be "forever" since defense of these laws seems always to overpower the will to regulate. This should suggest that regulatory statutes must be carefully drawn, but many are not. The attitude of most politicians seems to be the urge to draft a vague general law conveying sweeping powers and with no sense of limitation, often to show that they "have done something". This then provides a platform for forcing outside interest groups to come begging to them to negotiate the consequences. The results of these protracted negotiations are then "sealed" into the basic law, which tends to accrete endless immutable detail.

In most governments, the tendency in regulation is highly centrist, but where there are regional and municipal governments, it is their desire to have some regulatory authority of their own, to accommodate regulation to local circumstances. But the centrist government argues "if it is right to enforce a regulation, it is right that it be enforced all over the country with uniformity and little latitude for variation." It has long been reasoned that the political capital is best expended in passing a single national law, instead of permitting regulatory variations to exist at lower levels of government.

Regulation vs. Market Competition

The promotion of competition in market places is a concept much admired by economists, but often viewed by politicians with fear and loathing. Two major trends in the economic policies of governments following WW II were actively opposed to market competition, and to implement these policies, a wide range of regulations were developed. First, politicians sought to control the entry of foreign goods into the U. S. as a means to protect the markets served by American firms. This approach remains an evergreen for politicians who can be on both sides of the import argument, and this evergreen is alive and well in the American political scene, including the current Trump presidential administration. It should be noted that the extraordinary development of the "IT Revolution" was almost totally by private enterprise, and that it was vigorously competitive and not constrained by any government control. Regulation is increasingly seen as a negative resistance to change.

Second, the volume and value of contracts issued by governments has enormously expanded to the point that it has become an extremely important component of the total economy. It is therefore not surprising that regulations controlling the deployment of government contracts are also very important and highly sensitive. It is not coincidental that one of the most serious arenas of government corruption in the world – bribery, kickbacks, and bid rigging, over billing, and downright theft – has been in the murky world of government contracting.

One area in which economists and politicians seemed to have been on the same wavelength was the need for full disclosure of economic risks, and information about the financial strengths and weaknesses of economic enterprises. For economists, disclosure is seen as a prerequisite for rational economic decision making. For politicians, disclosure is seen as critical to the protection of the public from unknown risks. Yet the facts seem to be that disclosure which is so popular in theory has been largely neglected in practice, because, politicians fear the revealing of failure, and among the corrupt, disclosure is deadly. Governments themselves and their SOEs are notorious for the ominous secrecy of their information.

Regulation of Social Risk

Regulations tend to fall into two broad categories – economic and social. Economic regulation is universal because it relates so significantly to the broader issues of economic development. Social services regulation has had its greatest impact in developed nations, especially the United States. In addition to the more traditional health and safety regulation, a powerful new wave of environmental and conservation concerns has triggered the proliferation of regulations in these arenas. Social services regulations now increasingly deal with social imperatives such as racial equity, gender equity and the rights of gays and lesbians. These regulations tend to have high public acceptance and support and are relatively free of corrupt practices. Environmental protections had often been neglected not only because of their costs and the complexities of their enforcement but because they were regarded as creating negative inhibitions to some form of industrial or commercial development. But industrial waste may be dumped into lakes and rivers because it is deemed too expensive to dispose of them properly. Power companies pollute the air with effluents from their smoke stacks because they do not want to bear the costs of cleaner but more expensive fuels.

It is not unusual therefore to find that the legal or regulatory base is handsomely enunciated and defended in broad fine sounding commitments but falls far short of achieving such promises. Each regulation requires often very complex and expensive enforcement which has seldom been fully achieved, since it is far easier to write a regulation than it is to see to it that it is enforced. In the United States, the official Code of Federal Regulations, with 50 huge chapters, now contains an overwhelming 178,000 pages.

There is extensive regulation now of the banking system. Bank lending is vital to economic growth, and for the operations of both businesses and individuals. So it is proper to regulate to prevent bank system collapse or massive abuse. But the Moderate Party may want to define a clearer delineation between big international banks and more than 5,000 small local banks. Banks earned $56 Billion in profits in 2018, up 28% from 2017. The GOP is officially anti-regulation in general, and banks in particular. Democrats are in favor of "no retreat" from sturdy regulation of monster banks.

THE MODERATE PARTY AGENDA

1. First and foremost: The Moderate Party should stoutly defend the primacy of individual and organizational self-reliance in American life, and it should resist any excessive or unwarranted expansion of the range and depth of government regulation.
2. It must be realized that regulatory power is also regulatory control, and the Party should protect against its unwarranted expansion and extrapolation.
3. Regulation is also then one of the most powerful and dangerous sources of government corruption, and every regulation should have specific measures to protect its integrity.
4. The philosophical basis for all regulation should be facilitation, and enablement, and not opposition, limitation, and prohibition.
5. Regulations defined in law are widely extrapolated by their implementation in administrative procedures and processes. This has the consequence of in effect shifting law-making power to agency managers and administrators. The Party should demand that laws effectively limit such power to extrapolate.
6. In a similar vein, the reality is that the whole body of government regulation is already out of hand. The U. S. government official Code of Federal Regulations already contains 178,000 pages, and each of several thousand regulatory authorities has hundreds of thousands of supplemental "instructions". The is an overwhelming need to avoid this overwhelming.
7. For every regulation, there is the official mandate for its enforcement. When the actual demands that such enforcement would require is examined, thousands are seen as what they really are: missions impossible. Some major regulations apply to every citizen; where is the huge and ponderous government agency that would reach 328 million citizens, and who could afford its cost?

CONCERN FOR THE
ENVIRONMENT

"Global" environmentalism is now a world force politically, scientifically, and socially. Human warming of the climate is real, and it is not certain that there are adequate means to deal with it. We cannot create a perfect world, in the environment or in anything else. It is legitimate to ask - can we really control the environment, or can we even hope to prevent or mitigate the most urgent threats? Much is still essentially pompous rhetoric and phony wishful thinking. Note that there are now more than 7.6 BILLION people in the world, and this alone has created a major increase of energy consumption and an extraordinary increase in the importance of the critical uses of energy. It is fatuous beyond belief to make the base point for assessment the ancient world before the Industrial Revolution. It is foolish to make a time frame for planning the end of the century, more than 80 years from now. The Green New Deal now afloat in American politics is a phantom that has never been characterized or explained, and it is seriously improper and dangerous to try and sell it to the public. Nevertheless, the threat remains real.

It has been demanded that the U. S. must reach "zero carbon emission" in ten years, but there is absolutely no explanation about what would happen to 250 million private vehicles, or 133 million trucks, or 137 million private residences, or the whole system of electricity generation and use. Older readers may remember that the noted scientist Paul Ehrlich issued a book in 1968 entitled "The Population Bomb" which predicted that "hundreds of millions will starve to death"by the 70's because the supply of food would simply be overwhelmed by the huge surge and in world population. Or perhaps we will remember the MIT report which decided in 1972 that the world economy would collapse and civilization would fail because of "inevitable depletion of critical nonrenewable resources including natural gas and oil, aluminum, lead, tin, copper, zinc and even gold." Fifty years later we are still here and so are adequate supplies of all of these metals.

In the heating up of the science-based debate, people seem to forget that the object need not be the elimination of the 250 million private automobiles, or the 133 million trucks or the 133 million private residents or all of the national industrial base, or even the forced elimination of all producers of energy. The real target must be THE ELIMINATION OF THE SOURCES OF CARBON DIOXIDE. The real hope then is that new technical solutions will solve this problem without having to spend $13 trillion to eliminate fossil fuel use. In Europe, there is a government-led technology revolution, with the cost of solar photovoltaic systems falling by a factor of almost ten. The cost of wind systems offshore in the North Sea has been cut in half. As reported in the Washington Post of June 5, 2019, "The European Union's carbon pricing system has been successfully strengthened, contributing over the past decade to a halving of carbon dioxide emissions from U. K. electricity, and a 30 percent reduction in German hard coal consumption." Groups are now blossoming among people in agriculture to expand the pace of carbon removal through a variety of agricultural techniques; the massive reforestation of trees and shrubs; replanting after the cash crop has been harvested; composing, mulching, crop rotation, and less tilling generally. In some cases, public subsidies are being paid to encourage farm participation in these "capture and bury" types of programs

People are hard pressed to meet their urgent real needs, and not the temperature 80 years from now. There is a real concern about poverty and the lack of public services and infrastructure. They do not need a government that wants to beggar them in the name of global warming. And they expect their governments to develop more rational and realistic solutions. The further reality is that far too many governments are in serious disarray, totally incapable of dealing with the massive changes that even a 2 degree temperature decline would require.

But at least, note that the US use of energy is essentially flat, despite the increase of population to 328 million. Would the Moderate Party have to lurch into "mission impossible" – control of the lives and actions of more than 328 million people here, seven billion people in the world, and millions of people's organizations and actions? The Party should decide that the answer does not lie in the endless generation of controls – laws, regulations, enforcements, and law suits. Nor should it back the urge toward excess – e. g. "the regulation of ditches and puddles" or "protection of billions of bugs and birds". The scientific evidence about global warming is being degraded and threatened by the stupendous nonsense of the The Green New Deal and other hysterics.

An interesting example of convoluted thinking is represented by the lesson of U. S. national parks. The Obama Administration expanded the numbers and size of national parks, but at the same time, it was widely known that the entire parks system is in bad shape. Parks face a $11.6 billion backlog of maintenance and repair. This is a perfect and embarrassing example of the lack of courage of politicians. All along, the political leadership should have had the courage to raise the necessary funds, either by taxation, or by requiring higher park fees to be spent on maintenance.

In fact, the United States can point to many important advances in crucial environmental arenas: more energy efficient vehicles, changes in construction materials and protections, better fuel sources, more use of renewables, rapid growth in the use of LEDs and energy efficient batteries, solar panels, wind power, and new technology for natural gas extraction. It is critical to note that, while the government is slow to act, what has really been accomplished has been by millions of organizations and individual people in the country. There are ways to protect against the threats of extraction technology, and the use of coal continues to be driven down.

One of the dilemmas that a Moderate Party would face if in office would be to reexamine the American relationship to the environmental Paris Agreement. It certainly seems that there is a real sense of U. S. momentum in environmental concerns, and these advances would exist if there was no Paris Agreement at all. Are the goals of the Agreement more than rhetoric? There is a world-wide estimate of the threat of warming up to 3.3% Celsius by the end of the century which has generated a UN goal for constraining the decrease to below 2%. Yet even this target is seen by many serious analysts as mission impossible, phony and blatantly political. The so-called scientific reaction? Change the world "goal" from 2% to 1.5%!

Even the 2% goal would require huge changes beyond reality. The growing sophistication of modern societies has greatly enhanced energy demand, as for example, increases of more than 200% in Asia between 2006 and 2016. India expects its demand for energy to triple between 2016 and 2050. Everybody agrees that the uses of coal have to be curbed, but it is proving almost impossible in India, China and many other countries, including Germany. Huge sectors of the economy are coal dependent: steel, cement, transportation, farming and especially energy production. As a result, despite endless political promises, the use of coal has not shrunk for the last twenty years. The implacable reality is that the demands of hundreds of millions of lives will simply overpower vastly inadequate attempts at the reduction of energy use. A study done for the government of Maryland reported that the full development of just wind power alone would cost more than $1.4 billion. Further, the estimated cost of a full replacement of the current U. S. electric power system would about an incredible $5 Trillion, and this does not even include the added costs of changes that would have to be made inside buildings and homes. Nor does it include the costs to reconfigure the industrial and transportation systems themselves. The full estimate to gut the current national fossil fuel-based economy would be up to an utterly incomprehensible $13 TRILLION! In comparison, the total estimated cost for the U. S. to pursue WWII was about $4.3 trillion. The recommendation of the Maryland study was for the evolution, at some rational pace, of a system combining a natural gas base, supplemented by a range of renewable energy sources.

Increasingly, the world is really trying. There is a real honest sense in America of movement toward new technology, and more effective utilization of all means, in part driven by the fact that 61% of Americans see climate change as a serious threat. It now appears that there is a great surge of our 27 million businesses of all types and sizes to find ways to reduce their energy expenditures. There are far more solar panels in use; more wind turbines; more low-carbon technologies; more electric cars. In fact, big car makers around the world and especially in China have invested heavily in conversions of some of their production to manufacture of electric cars, driven in large part by an exceptional upgrading of battery technology. According to Bloomberg New Energy Finance, American auto makers may reach 15% of sales by 2025. As a compelling example, the government of the city of Shenzen in China has undertaken a project to convert all city buses and taxis to all-electric sources. Using heavy subsidies from the national government, the city has spent more than $60 billion to date to replace more than 16,000 buses and about 12,000 taxis, and shifted official city vehicles for the police, fire departments and postal service. In addition, the city with heavy national government support has installed hundred of thousands of charging stations around the city.

Slowly but perceptively, the American development of some form of carbon tax is gaining traction, and more people are willing to see pressure brought to bear on generators of carbon into the atmosphere. The premise is that the tax penalty will force organizations to work harder on carbon intervention. An attractive idea would be to use this tax revenue not as an addition to government revenue, but as funds placed into some form of government "revenue neutral" account which is paid to consumers themselves in the form of a tax rebate or income tax adjustment, which could be slanted to favor low income people. It is true that President Clinton was unable to pass such a tax in 1993, nor could President Obama get one thru in 2009, but the hope is that the public opinion tide has shifted by increasing concern about the environment so that such an attractive idea is now feasible.

And there is an increasing willingness to rely on an old solution – the use of nuclear energy. There has been a substantial relaxation of national resistance to nuclear power generation. The U. S. now realizes more than 20% of it its generated power from nuclear sources, which is now the second largest source after coal. (coal = 38.3%; gas = 23.1%; hydro = 16.6%; oil =3.7%). The country now has 98 operable nuclear power plants.

The United States is now the largest producer of nuclear power generation the world. And most of these technologies, as they advance, are becoming simpler and cheaper. The costs of electricity from wind and solar sources have plunged by about 70% and 90% respectively. Anti-carbon attacks have advanced far beyond energy generation and have extended into economic sectors such as steel and aluminum production, transport, cement and the whole farming world.

These changes are a triumph from the "bottom up" world that the Moderate Party should latch on to. There is an increasing understanding that the real target is not to get rid of energy users, or energy generators, but to eliminate the sources of carbon dioxide. Thus, the expansion of the various methods for carbon prevention and capture must be taken by the Moderate Party as Goal Number One. The pattern seems to be far greater use of nuclear sources, supplemented by the much expanded use of non-fossil renewable sources and far more aggressive development of carbon capture technology to get at the real problem.

THE MODERATE PARTY AGENDA

1. First and foremost, the real goal of party policy is to work to eliminate the generation of carbon dioxide; not to destroy users of power, but to

clear the air. We cannot, and should not attempt to destroy millions of cars, millions of trucks, and the national energy production system. The case for the development of a new carbon tax is complex, but warrants careful evaluation.

2. The Party would be a strong promotor of all forms of energy efficiency technology, involving both public enterprise and governments.

3. We should support readily available improvements in agricultural production which can be adapted and enhanced by millions of farmers and agricultural businesses.

4. The Moderate Party must act to restore the public acceptance of nuclear power generation since it is the single greatest potential generator of carbon free energy.

5. The Green New Deal must be opposed unless and until it is fully explained, and a rational explanation provided as to how it might be undertaken —without destroying much of the country.

6. The party will face a confrontation with the UN over the Paris Energy Agreement. Is it a sensible formula for huge and hugely expensive objectives for fossil energy reduction, or is it simply another politicized expression of false goals and false hopes?

7. Collateral to this is the grim reality that half of the governments in the world are in deep trouble in political, economic, and social terms. They are absolutely incapable of the management of mammoth restructuring of the world economy - when most have trouble providing basics like food and shelter.

EFFECTIVE GOVERNMENT OPERATIONS

The Moderate Party would be a powerful mechanism to reverse what has been a quiet but perfectly visible tide that has been running in governments at all levels for the last 50 years or more. This is the tendency for the public and our political leadership to preoccupy themselves with the political conflicts and debates and to ignore the serious responsibility of governments to operate effectively. In other words, "politics vs. management" has become another form of conflict within government, with the knowledge that management has been losing out to politics, much of it bad, and that bad politics inevitably produces bad management. Governments at all levels have become larger, more important in national affairs, more complex, less comprehensible, and very, very, very much more expensive. An enormous increase in the demands being placed on the governance system demands a much-enhanced ability to manage these more extensive and complicated affairs. But, to a disturbing degree, this higher level of managerial competence has not materialized or has been politically ignored.

But the American public has genuine right to expect their governments to function at a high level under such critical concepts as "efficiency" and "effectiveness" and "high productivity". Further, the public is entitled to expect that governments should actually know what they are doing and why; and that the result of each program is realistically known and that the money spent is actually producing good results. Where program improvements may be needed or loser programs or projects should be reduced or eliminated, it is expected that managers will actually doing these things so that the public demands for effective management of government programs are really being met. The public may also have the reasonable expectation that governments will tell the truth, prevent corruption and theft, and work always to serve the public and not just their friends and supporters. In other words, the great tradition of honest and effective management must be recognized by both the American public and by the political leadership that good management is a proper and vital necessity.

What is good management? The answer is widely understood. It is taught in universities. It is learned on the job. It is absorbed and understood by millions of people at all levels as their profession and obligation. Does the federal government of the United States, and our thousands of state, county and municipal governments provide such good and professional management? The answer seems to be "yes, but ------".

To begin with, the totality of the national government system is unbelievably huge and complex, sophisticated, complicated, muddled and notoriously fragmented and yet interrelated. There is no such thing as "the government" since we have literally hundreds of governments, program by program and place by place. This vast complex has never been a coherent entity designed to be "managed" as that term is understood in other contexts. There are three starting points from which to evaluate government. The first is from the top down, which is the way the most politicians and most news media look at the world. The second way is from the middle down, which is where the U.S. middle class and the Moderate Party lives. The third basis for evaluation of governance if from the bottom up. This is not just the needy; it is often the people who have such serious concerns about their governments that they are driven actively to seek urgent reforms.

Governance from the top down is how almost every government works. From the top down, governments are created and designed not for management effectiveness but for political advantages, and as discussed earlier, the political view of the world is often markedly different from the professional management view.

The President is "the top". By order of the Constitution, he is the Chief Executive of the government, and yet not even the President can really manage the totality the way a chief executive of corporations can manage. But the President does have the power now to appoint about 4,000 top level political appointees, plus effective control of another 2,000 non-political government officers. Still, much of the operational power and authority for specific government programs is vested by law not in the President but in the head of the government agency that delivers the program. Cabinet secretaries and agency heads may "work for" the President and be appointed by him, but each also "works for" the Congress because of a very complex legal base of authorizing and defining legislation, and continued oversight which can determine agency policy, and define the agency's structure, fix many of its processes, and ultimately control its finances. The President cannot order his leaders to violate the law and should be careful not to try.

So, we go back to the interpretation of the civil servant's managerial obligation. Clearly, it is not just to be the sacred principles of classic professional management as taught in universities and corporate board rooms. It is a deeper and more compelling and more confusing form of management, carrying both specialized legal and moral obligations. But it must be understood that the role of every government agency is vastly complex and sophisticated, going far beyond mere paper shuffling. There is therefore a mandate placed on every person in a position of authority in governments to make a maximum commitment to producing valuable and cost-effective management for the American public, and this mandate applies to politicians as well to work for government effectiveness and not just getting reelected.

Over a long period of U. S. governance, the reputation of public managers has, in fact, been reassuringly high. The provision of effective government is perhaps the most difficult thing that nations are called upon to do. Often, political leadership has proven to be disturbingly bad, pursuing policies and relationships that create conflict and reduce the capacity for the government's managers to function effectively. It is vital that every U. S. government recognize and try to live up to their obligation to be effective – both in political and managerial terms. All of the tools for achieving effectiveness exist; what seems to be lacking is the will and the courage to use them up to their real potential. It would be one of the most important different attitudes fostered by the Moderate Party: to fully value this commitment for effective government management, in the face of prejudiced political resistance if necessary.

One of the central dilemmas of American governments at all levels has become a system in which **special interests** have come to dominate the provision of funds and influence for political campaigns, which in turn translates into the creation of hundreds of government programs designed to favor these special interests organizations, often at some cost to the general public interest. Each of these special interest programs becomes locked into law, and they are then stoutly defended against any elimination, retrenchment or even reform. The legislation is, by design, so detailed that it blocks any capacity for managerial innovation. Then, the special interest groups will invariably continue to press for new increments of preferment and subsidy. It cannot be overstated; if the Moderate Party is created to have the courage to reform government failures, ONE OF ITS MOST IMPORTANT AND URGENT OBJECTIVES MUST BE TO FACE UP TO THE PERVERSIONS OF SPECIAL INTEREST POLITICS AND RETURN THE POLITICAL SYSTEM INTO THE HANDS OF OUR GENERAL PUBLIC. PERIOD.

Among the upper levels of the civil service, this special interest ascendency is particularly disturbing. For them, reality is that the world is always changing, and managers must be free to accommodate to such changes. Programs become marginal, less valuable, overly expensive, or simply obsolete. New demands for government action emerge, but cannot be responded to. And career managers are increasingly unwilling to press for management reforms in the face of implacable, and often threatening and dangerous political resistance. In this special interest world, there seems to be virtually no political capacity to say "no" to anybody, and government priorities may be based on preferment for friendly special interests, rather than on public need or value. A look at the published lists of Washington lobbyists reveals the extraordinary number and range of the beneficiaries of this system. A look at the budgets of Federal, state and local governments shows thousands of budget line items financing these business and social advocacy interests. State and local governments in turn have become huge special interests in themselves, drawing funds from Federal programs ranging from health, education and environmental protection, to law enforcement, fire protection, road construction and maintenance and many forms of tax advantages.

What is the effective course of action for the Moderate Party to pursue against this perversion? It lies in a deliberate effort, from largely public sources, to **educate the general public** about the dilemma of special interest politics, and officially encourage the public to speak out against special interest perversions. Public distress over government, and especially political failure does seem get the public increasingly reacting to what it perceives as the decline in government effectiveness and thus the performance and reputation of the government's corps of professional executives and managers.

GOVERNMENT CONTRACTS AND GRANTS

One of the most important dimensions of government operations has become that of contract management.Every agency of federal, state, county and city governments is a user of contracts, starting with the most mundane such as the collection of trash, or security guard services, up to extraordinarily complex contracts for space exploration and weapons system development.

> The management of government grants and contracts is probably the single most important arena for the exercise of better government management.

For many governments, the use of contracts may be a matter of choice or a matter of necessity. There has been a long term controversy over those who argue the careful reliance on the utilization of full civil service employees, both as legal protection of the rights and interests of governments and as a skilled and relatively inexpensive source of talent. The counter argument is based on the undoubted fact that there are many goods and services that governments can best obtain from contractor organizations.

In any event, the use of government contracting is so extensive that governments have, of necessity, evolved a whole complete and elaborate set of laws, regulations and managerial systems for selection and management of government contracts. The role of the manager is to contract for the right things, at the right price, and a satisfactory level of performance. Yet there is a vastly disturbing record of the mismanagement of such contracts and the failure to contract with the best bidding company. Then, once under contract, the government can be billed for things not really delivered; for goods and services that are overpriced; for "ghost" workers and activities; for services never delivered; and for plain old fashioned lying and cheating. Both politicians and managers are guilty of these sins.

Once a contractor begins work under a contract, whole new forms of corruption become possible. The work itself can be pathological: shoddy work, substandard materials, failure to perform required work, unwarranted expenses, overstated costs, deliberate cost overruns, and many more failures. Cost may be overstated. The government may be billed "phantom charges" for work or supplies not actually provided. The workforce may be overstated and phantom wages and benefits billed to the government. Work delays may be deliberately created to pump up costs. Management salaries or overhead costs may be excessive. Unfortunately the contractor may feel that the quality of government oversight is so poor that such illegalities will never be caught. In other cases kickbacks are simply made to public officials to turn a blind eye to such cheating. Government managers and inspectors may not be competent, or may be too few to cover all contracts. Performance is not evaluated, costs are not verified, goods are "lost" or stolen, and accounts are not audited. Where a contractor is caught in an illegal or improper act, the overseeing government official may be bribed or coerced to ignore the fact. Even the protections of auditors or inspectors may be frustrated through bribes or political pressure. Just because some activities are performed under contract does not reduce the responsibility of government contract managers for the activities themselves.

Contracts usually state that the government commits to paying all legitimate costs plus a reasonable fee, fixed in advance. A somewhat more sophisticated approach may be used where the government pays all legitimate costs, plus an award fee which may go up if performance is better than expected. When the government is buying routine things such as office supplies or equipment it may just purchase from the most convenient source, but even here, if the government is purchasing large volumes of material or services, a contract competition is far better. In any event, the government is responsible for spelling out a specific set of rules and regulations that define its relationships with contractors. These rules are different from the rules that govern the government civil service. For example, contracts are not governed by the government's system for determination of employee pay and benefits, but by their own corporate pay system.

The single most effective curb against contract corruption continues to be the mandated use of competitive bidding. A carefully drafted law mandating competition can be used as the basis for defending agency contracting practices, and giving leverage to reformers and those officials in agencies who genuinely want fair and legal contracting to prevail. But a legislative mandate for competition even if it is achieved, is far from enough.

Each agency of government should be required to supplement the law with a carefully defined and published set of procedures for bid competition. The initial contractor selection process is critical because it is here that the likelihood of corruption will first manifest itself. If bad public officials and companies seize the contract at this point, it is likely that subsequent operations under the contract will be a constant problem. All contract bids should be subjected to an opaque evaluation process aimed at getting a realistic assessment of bidder capabilities. This evaluation should be open to review, at least for auditors and other bidders to examine. That way, if a selecting official makes a decision that runs counter to the technical evaluation; such an arbitrary selection can be more effectively challenged.

During the performance of each contract, there should be multiple responsibilities. First, the official in charge of the contract must be made clearly responsible for its effective management. This is the first and most important line of defense against impropriety, and no amount of post audit can substitute for it. This responsibility includes real time determination that the demands of the contract are being met, that only authorized work is performed and billed, that all costs are realistic and appropriate, and that costly overruns are avoided. In support of these contract managers may be allies in the agency who will audit, inspect or investigate contractor performance if necessary. These government oversight systems should extend down to subcontractors or suppliers of the prime contractor.

To its credit, the U. S. government in its official roles has always taken this series of contract problems seriously, and it maintains a generally effective range of official mechanisms to press for effective contract supervision. Compared to about 120 other governments, ours is a model of rectitude. If there is an arena where better performance is needed, it is in the ability of the government to ferret out full understanding of contractor costs to permit a more forceful detection of excessive costs beyond reality, or the billing of improper costs, the inventions of "ghost" charges, or simple thievery. The government seems to need to consult some housewives to learn how to shop – meaning to purchase the goods or services that are the most value for money, and not those that are merely lazy or convenient.

If one looks at the performance of governments around the world, U. S. governments remain among the best in the world, and American citizens really have much to be proud of in the performance of their governments. The public administration community is seriously lacking in its ability to explain to the public all of the things that governments do well and effectively. In truth, the government's managers probably do better at their jobs than many politicians do in theirs. It is important for the public and the public administration community itself to **speak out** against the kind of bad politics that forces bad management. The Moderate party must argue that governments should be able to rid themselves of programs and activities that are useless, of low value, or simply obsolete. Managers need more latitude to eliminate overlap and duplications in public programs, or to do away with mandated regulations that are overly complicated, too intrusive, time-wasting, costly and often simply pointless. Managers often know when some program is costing a lot and achieving little, or other programs that produce more harm than good. Part of this political problem is the tendency of politicians to put the blame for faltering pubic program performance on "the bureaucracy" (not us politicians!) and to assert that the government is "too large", ignoring the fact that it is the political leadership that made it so.

It is true that the federal government has grown enormously in the last 40 years in terms of size, range of authority, cost and numbers of programs. The government now involves around 1,000 identifiable programs of increased complexity. In 1970, the federal budget was just around $200 million. It reached $1 trillion in 1987, and it has now topped $3.6 trillion. That means that it is more than 17 times larger, and even allowing for inflation, it is a powerful statement of the magnitude and sophistication of the government that our federal executives and managers are expected to manage.

But meanwhile, the population of the federal civil service, which peaked at 6.6 million in 1968, is now down to about 4.2 million – an absolute decline of 37% since 1968. These figures provide a telling story of how the government has changed, and if they were better understood, they would be a powerful statement about the real effectiveness of the government and its leaders.

In summary, Federal, state and local governments have become huge, complex and highly sophisticated groups of institutions that create demands for effective management far beyond the political layer at the top. The American public is right to expect these governments to employ the very best of professional management and leadership, and it is the responsibility of the career leadership to fight for an environment that supports and facilitates excellence in management instead of ignoring or even frustrating it.

It is easy to say that this pattern must be reversed, but it is far from clear how, especially since the two dominant political parties are partners in creating the problems, much less in trying to mitigate them, and this is one of the most powerful incentives for creating a Moderate Party alternative. The Moderate Party would galvanize the whole professional civil service to advocate and defend the importance of managerial competence and effectiveness to be pushed with greater seriousness across the whole range of government activities. Bland utterances of political and agency leadership are not and never have been enough. More support for quality management leadership must come from the bottom up as well as better from the top down. What is needed is a longer-term program to reform the organization and management of government agencies: to simplify, eliminate, speed up and create a greater attention to cost effectiveness.

Over the years, a number of very interesting proposals have been advanced for reforming the overblown structures of government. For example, the lives of farm families are now more stable, and farm families are able now to take care of themselves. Do we need therefore, to continue our enormous and elaborate and costly subsidization of farmer and agricultural businesses? Almost certainly not, and a drastic reorganization and reduction of the Department of Agriculture is warranted along with the elimination of dozens of costly agricultural industry subsidies.

There is a good case to simply privatize the Postal Service and let it compete with the many private sector shipping companies. It has been argued that the Air Traffic Control system should be taken out of the Federal Aviation Administration (FAA) and converted to a private corporation selling its services to air carriers and air ports. Would it be possible to simplify social services by creating a single broader Health and Public Welfare Department, merging in the current Education and Labor Departments? Remember why these two departments got created in the first place; to cater to the interests of education and union organizations. By some miracle, would it be possible to thin out the layers and layers and layers of government departments and divisions and offices and branches, one on top of the other?

The Moderate Party could become the greatest source of serious advocacy for government reorganization and management reform in the United States today.

THE MODERATE PARTY AGENDA

1. Make all policy debates include provisions to enhance the effectiveness of government operations.
2. Demand more efforts to rank and set priorities for all governments, and eliminate or reduce those that are useless or of marginal value.
3. Require government managers to evaluate the value of their programs with the intent to eliminate or reduce those of low productivity.
4. Galvanize the key people among the Civil Service to get them to manage more effectively, and to provide more information to educate the American public.
5. Implacably oppose the perversions of special interest politics and eliminate those cases that adversely impact the general public.

6. Avoid adverse political meddling against effective government operations, since bad politics results in bad management.
7. Lead and enforce government-wide attacks on the sins of fraud, waste, mismanagement, abuse of authority, or simple incompetence.
8. Lead and enforce a strong continuing attack on government corruption.

THE ART OF BAD BUDGETING

To a very serious extent, the nature of governance and its reputation rests on what emerges in the formal budgets of each department and agency. The content of an agency budget is defined by two categories: first is the programs and projects that the agency administers; and second is the "overhead" costs of agency personnel, its buildings and facilities, and its operational services such as power and transportation. Of these two, the far more complex budget development deals with the program base.

The development of program costs is not easy, and often it is perverse. If the public sees this as a simple process carried out on an adding machine, it is much deluded. The preparation of an agency budget is an art form of exquisite complexity, played from agency back rooms all the way up to the White House and the halls of Congress. Government budgeting starts from the bureaucratic bottom up. The mid level program manager will start the process, and his/her motives may be quite complicated. The manager will assume that one of the prime motives for his superiors will be to appear fiscally prudent, and thus, each will appear to "cut" some funding to demonstrate such prudence. Thus, the middle manager will almost certainly inflate his/her initial estimates to neutralize the anticipated cuts. Some may not actually know what the program will cost because of inflation and the crafty managers of program recipient organizations. But at the same time, it may be also the desire of managers to portray the program as a "success" by portraying the need for more money to support success. These earnest budget offerings are then passed upward through two channels; first, the line of command from boss to boss; and then through a "Budget Office" and other staff reviewers, whose roles are to be suspicious and negative.

In general, two criteria are important. One hopefully seeks to put the available money into the program elements that will have real impact and value. Second is to put the money where it will create the most political satisfaction. Agency budgets are advanced to the President through the Office of Management and Budget (OMB) which plays several roles. First, it collects and consolidates the budgets from all of the agencies and forges them into something called "The President's Budget". In this process, OMB will conduct a content evaluation of each agency budget, hoping to squeeze out the trash, threaten the gamers, sustain the important and vital budget needs, and strike the "right" balance between the managerially desirable and the politically feasible. OMB issues budget guidance at the start of each budget cycle that defines presidential goals, objectives, targets, and inhabitions. OMB works for the presidency, not for the agencies or for Congress. In recent years, its role has been extended to give more attention to achieving government-wide encouragement of high quality management, justified as a means for maximizing budget effectiveness. At the same time, it has been made more of a political instrument on behalf of the President, pushing and often defining political control of budget allocation.

The President and OMB prepare the President's Budget which is submitted to the appropriations committees of the Congress, and here another reality sinks in. By Constitutional mandate, the federal government budget is ultimately the instrument of the Congress and not just of the President. There is always a titanic clash between the two over the ultimate budget that will emerge. In some years, this conflict has been so great that the presidential budget is said to be "dead on arrival". Conflicts are over policy, interpretations of program effectiveness, special interest political preferment, local government political influence, and the amounts of money (or debt) available for spending. Nobody—absolutely nobody – can predict the final outcome at the end of this dance.

What then would constitute "good" budgeting? One marvelous goal would be a whole major simplification and rationalization of the whole budget structure itself, with hundreds of fewer bits and pieces, more multi-year budgets for known, stable programs, and a deliberate effort to throw out the trash, including repugnant special interest payoffs, notorious earmarking, and the elimination of programs and projects whose legal authorization has expired. What is argued here is the high budget value of effective program management vs. the low value of political bargaining, cunning and payoff.

It seems also clear that it is very important to maintain and even strengthen two critical institutions: the Office of Management and Budget, in the Executive Office of the President; ; and the Government Accountability Office, which is an instrumentality of the Congress. Both represent a critical back pressure within the budget/policy world. Somebody has to say "Not so fast!", or "Prove it!". OMB works for the President, but in the larger and more statesmanlike sense, it really works for the institutional presidency. GAO clearly works for the Congress, but in that more statesmanlike sense, it really works for the legislative branch of government.

Through many credible assessments, a list of potential program eliminations would be developed. Here is such a list.

1. DOD: base closings
2. DOD: marginal weapons systems.
3. DOD: structure of pay, benefits, health insurance, retirement benefits.
4. Agriculture subsidies: eliminate entirely; or limit to small farm operations.
5. Eliminate all corporate marketing, overseas subsidies.
6. Catch more deadbeats
7. Catch more cheaters.
8. Eliminate organizational overlap, duplication, redundancy, obsolete programs, high cost/low value programs.
9. Institute a hiring freeze on government employment; but this must be accompanied by a similar freeze on contractor employment.
10. Freeze employee raises in salary and benefits for some fixed time. Hold back COLA dates, amounts.
11. Freeze the appropriations for most domestic programs; exempt a very limited number of appropriations such as Social Security or troop operations.
12. Freeze additional spending of funds authorized by the 2010 stimulus program.
13. Eliminate/reduce federal subsidies for higher education.
14. Restrict Pell grants to the truly needy.
15. Eliminate subsidies to local governments for AMTRAK, roads, mass transit, airports, law enforcement, school facilities, community development, etc.

16. Eliminate government R & D that can/should be done by the private sector.

17. Put a cap on government overhead; mandate a cost reduction program for all agencies. Failure to achieve voluntary results could trigger a mandated fund cut.

Is this the basis for a possible set of budget forms? Not likely.

THE MODERATE PARTY AGENDA

1. Given the lack of courage and common sense in determining the validity of the budget, the Moderate Party reluctantly would support mandating a balanced budget by law; an option not recommended might be a Constitutional amendment with a provision that the limit amount cannot be changed for a fixed number of years.

2. This in turn would require enactment of a budget cap for each year, with the provision that any appropriation that would exceed the cap must be accompanied by some equal reduction elsewhere in the budget.

3. Devolution of programs to states where it is the logical performer, and such a devolution would convey federal funding plus state or city funding.

4. This creates two bureaucracies for each program – Federal and State – and endless conflict and confusion. The state is the proper level of control and administration for many programs where the federal role is mostly as a provider of largely supplemental money and overall policy direction. The Party would undertake to simplify the enormous complexity of management of these programs.

5. Purge the tax code of special interest breaks, and tax loopholes. This of necessity would be a very heavy, very serious and long term effort. The ferderal government budget would be one of the absolute prime targets for reform.

6. Consider the use of vouchers for education, Medicare, Medicaid. The general premise is that, instead of paying money to local government units, the money would be paid to individual citizens. For example, parents would be given vouchers to buy elementary education at schools of their choice, not necessarily the schools that the school

system assigns. Or patients would be given vouchers for medical care and they could choose where and how the money would be spent. This would be in direct and explicit opposition to the growing current support for some form of "Medicare For All".

7. Create a universal VAT system and use it to replace many current taxes, including some degree of individual income taxes.The VAT is seen as more equitable, easier and cheaper to administer, and, if properly valued, could generate an equal or greater amount of taxes relatively painlessly, like wage withholding.

8. Change federal government Medicaid payments from an open ended arrangement to a fixed block grant arrangement tied to population and overall inflation and not supposed health care costs.

9. End DOD weapon hoarding. The Moderate Party would have to take these potential future needs very seriously but it must back the general premise that DOD can and should pare back it urge to acquire.

10. The Moderate Party would face an ancient and highly pushed tendency to constantly increase government-provided services and assistance. The Only reality is that it must face up to the pressures for "more" and it must work hard to indentify and ativate limits on program benefits. The Moderate Party would mount a deliberate program to determine priorities between and among programs with the lowest priority activities either eliminated or drastically reduced.

THE NATIONAL SECURITY ESTABLISHMENT

The United States military establishment includes about 3300 combat aircraft, ten major aircraft carriers, 72 nuclear submarines and several hundred 68 ton Abrams tanks. It is becoming increasingly hard to justify the care and feeding of these huge complex weapons systems, or to understand where they would be used. These weapons are a holdover from the days when DOD argued that the U. S. might find itself fighting two major wars at the same time. This is no longer a feasible scenario, and we no longer need to "weaponize" for them. The past was around huge alliances of national military forces scaled to cooperate to fight huge wars. The future now is for each country to develop the police-like units to fight limited conflicts with domestic enemies and internationalized terrorist organizations. These units should be linked not to fight each other's enemies but to pursue enemies that are deliberately designed to fight and run, to sneak across borders, to attack static military posts, and then quickly to disappear. Most military personnel should now be army; fewer navy units, and more limited air units. The nature of weaponry must also change. OUT is the age of battleships and 68 ton tanks and high altitude bombers and maybe aircraft carriers. IN are sniper units, body armor, vehicle protection, explosives detection technology, small unit tactics, drones, hypersonic missiles, urban spy networks, and faster and smarter links between everybody's defense units.

In 2016, then Secretary of Defense Robert Gates issued a scathing assessment of American defense priorities, and his recommendation bear repeating in detail. He stated:

1. The U. S. should stop thinking – and spending –on **general deterrance** and concentrate on specific priority missions and specific tasks, and to shift from old conventional thinking in favor of more modern and realistic patterns of special operations against localized targets by combined and integrated forces.

2. It is increasingly apparent that the nature of military engagement has been changing away from major "world" war to smaller localized "neighborhood" conflict. As a consequence, DOD needs to **change its thinking** toward more small level integrated operations in which military personnel function more like police than heavy duty crushers.

3. The DOD must stop **loving every weapons system** and excessive and redundant capability. Gates cites many examples: the Marine Expeditionary Fighting Vehicle designed for amphibious landings – none of which have been conducted for the last 70 years; more F-35 fighters (at a cost of over $600 billion) when we already have more than we can use; a next generation attack submarine, when current U. S. subs are beyond attack already; the Medium Air Defense System, which is redundant with the current Patriot systems. After spending $ 130 billion on a ballistic missile defense system, an additional $ 30 billion is simply not needed or justified.

4. Specifically, DOD should drastically cut back the purchase of the **F-35 Lightning II aircraft.** Current F-15s, 16s and 18s are already the best in the world. "The Chinese M-20 is about at their level, but it is only "modestly" stealthy, especially from behind." The F-35 is justified because it will be used by all U. S military services, and many will be bought by other countries. But 180 have already been delivered, and each Service has insisted on specially designed versions for its own purposes. It is hard to pin down what the ultimate numbers are expected to be built; numbers as high as + 2400 have been reported. But it is almost certain that the ultimate cost will exceed $ 600 billion. The most recent purchase, for 90 aircraft, is scheduled to cost $8.2 billion.

5. Also, DOD should eliminate the **V-22 Osprey tilt rotor aircraft** program as prohibitively expensive, and the fact that its performance in Iraq and Afghanistn was "not impressive". DOD should also eliminate the preposterous blimp carried cruise missile surveillance system.

6. Similarly, the military already has a very large inventory of the **Abrams tanks** – perhaps the best in the world, but often not fully usable in modern "neighborhood" warfare. Future purchases of these tanks seems questionable.

7. Eleven huge **aircraft carriers**? They are increasingly difficult to protect, especially from ultra-long range hypersonic missiles, and they no longer seem justified. And three more are planned?

8. **Research but not production.** It would be perfectly feasible for the DOD to pursue a revised policy where it continues to undertake weapons systems research and development, so that it continues to have the best weapons systems in the world, but to avoid taking these weapons into the next step of production unless there is a clear and present need to make them operational. R & D is relatively cheap; production is very expensive.

9. **Inventory control.** Gates bemoans the fact that "current inventories of hundreds of thousands of items are already way beyond foreseeable need". Add the fact that other studies have reported that too many military warehouses are duplicating items in the four Services, and these warehouses maintain at great expense weapons no longer used, uniforms no longer issued, boots that nobody now wears, and much else that is useless and obsolete and redundant.

10. This logic extends beyond inventory to **the military bases themselves.** There are hundreds of them. Many of them are flatly unnecessary, and they could be closed and their activities performed elsewhere. Others are obsolete, inefficient, and overly expensive for the results they deliver. Others could be combined and consolidated. Again, where is the zeal and the courage to address these concerns?

11. **Human resources costs.** According to Gates: "human resources costs such as pay, benefits, health care and retirement funding have grown so much that 'they are eating the Defense Department alive'" The level of many benefits are seen as unrealistic. DOD, as much as any element of government, it still mired in a world of bureaucratic paperwork, an enormous and utterly debilitating structure of hundreds of organizational units of vague and often obsolete activities, endlessly running around in tight little circles pushing paper. Simplify! Thin down! Automate!

12. **Enormous bureaucracy.** Unfortunately, DOD is heavily over-organized, starting with the questionable continued need for four

separate Services, the seeming inability to produce truly integrated operations, the vast oceans of paperwork and paper shuffling, and concerns about overstaffing and the consequent huge costs of pay, benefits, and ultimately, retirement costs. And the needs for reform must necessarily extend down to the huge numbers of DOD contractors. The need for reform and restructuring cannot and should not be taken as any repudiation of the crucial role of the U. S. military in the world. Better can also mean more. The need? Again, SMALLER-SIMPLER-CHEAPER.

13. In the past, the American government has, through DOD programs, ended up **funding tyrants, dictators, and official thieves**. Many of these problems were defined and justified by the need to "oppose Communism". That rationalization has now gone away, and it is time for the DOD and the government as a whole to more carefully determine the nature of our "friends".

As these changes take place, the nature of the DOD physical establishment will change. DOD must address the current overwhelming muddle of military facilities and bureaucracy, and it must thin out the complex and questionable relationships with the military/industrial complex. There will be far less need for large, heavily staffed bases and facilities because more of the smaller, scattered assaults can be met by flying smaller defense units to the points of attack. DOD can and should phase out obsolete facilities, cancel obsolete programs and projects, deliberately eliminate or concentrate thousands of "offices" for this and that. It is disturbing to realize that, over many years, several Secretaries of Defense have repeatedly asked for more authority from Congress to close or cut back these bases and facilities. Secretary Mattis is the most recent, and he testified that perhaps 19% of DOD structure and facilities are "excess to need" and that "every unnecessary facility we maintain requires us to cut capabilities elsewhere. He testified that "I must be able to eliminate excess infrastructure in order to shift resources to more readiness and modernization". Why is Congress unwilling to act? It is held back by its political protection of local community income and heavily entrenched commitments to its thousands of contractors. This is one of the most blatant examples of how bad politics makes bad management.

It is now possible to believe that the threat of a major nuclear holocaust is very unlikely, and that the U. S. will never actually be a target for anybody. The growing complexity and interrelationships of even the shabbiest of country economies make diplomacy and the leverages of economic pressures the real means by which threats can be mitigated.

The second element of U. S. national security is in the form of its law enforcement system. This is in only limited ways a national system since thousands of law enforcement units function, as they should, almost totally on local levels. Perhaps the main question is to realize the increasing concern of people with police forces that do not function well enough in providing "help and protection", and too much on providing "enforcement and control". Yet both is exactly what people seem to want. There is a growing problem in urban areas over the country where police clash with parts of the urban population. One of the conflicting issues is the frequent failure of urban social services, which creates much of the citizen revulsion, which then slops over into blame on the police. Too many people end up in prisons for far too minor offences. Too many weapons are far too easily available. MS-13 gangs inexplicably flourish. Finally, there is the long-term reality of police corruption, usually in cities where there is a high level of political corruption in general. The police are seen as taking bribes, extorting citizens and businesses, using threats and intimidation, and threatening false arrest. Thus, it is surely one of the most demanding of obligations to design and implement a whole series of major reforms of these vital but deeply troubled public services.

THE MODERATE PARTY AGENDA

1. The Department of Defense has already begun the great and sophisticated transition from a military establishment based on huge numbers of troops deploying huge numbers of weapons to fight huge wars between nations. Hugeness is out, and the new wave is for each nation to mount forces capable of fighting smaller localized militia-like groups, that stand for nothing but the seizure of power, and are often terrorist in intent.

2. The U. S. in turn must shift its primary thrust to small multi-capability units able to mount integrated operations – fast and hard and anywhere.

3. The DOD then has a serious responsibility to stop spending on wars of general deterrence, and start spending on the new integrated military competence.

4. As a part of this change, the Party and the defense establishment must face up to the redesign of our military physical plant, supply and logistics structures, and indeed the whole now overblown bureaucracy. A smaller, simpler, cheaper, and faster organization must emerge.

5. R and D must continue, but it is likely now that the best course is follow the research to the point of development, but then not enter into the more expensive level of production unless it is clear that the new weapon is actually needed.

6. The other main element of national security is that of law enforcement. This only partly a national system, and it involves hundreds of local capabilities. There is a genuine issue of the conflict between police forces seeking to do their duty, and major elements of the urban population who see this as threatening and oppressive. The Party would work at several levels to "soften" the thrust of law enforcement. It is important to really believe that the police must "serve and protect", rather than prevent and control. This more supportive attitude must extend the political leadership as well.

7. And it should be recognized that much of the urban conflict stems from the lack of adequate social services in many communities. These failures often end up putting the law enforcement elements of cities in an unwarranted bad light.

8. But a real burden for law enforcement: its own corruption. This is not just the occasional free donut or cup of coffee. It involves bribery, extortion of citizens and businesses, threats, intimidation, and threats of false arrest. It would have to be one of the most important responsibilities of the Moderate Party to make major efforts to drive out this blight.

THE AMERICAN
INTERGOVERNMENTAL SYSTEM

One of the most compelling approaches to the restraint of centrist authoritarian governments is deliberately to press for the assignment or or delegation of authority over many government programs to regional (e. g. state, county, city) governments. There is a continuing debate about the kinds and levels of decentralization and devolution in governments. The central government is in charge of this debate, and will certainly guarantee its own power. Cities are de facto sources of power, and they will be the main sources of leverage for local government authority. Typically, the strongest views against devolution come from the centrist power holders, and from macroeconomists who believe that economic development is best when driven from the top. There is also a strong element of simple inertia, in part because many do not want to change the current allocation of power because they fear the added responsibility, or do not understand what to replace it with, and they do not want to face up to the need to do some heavy lifting in the face of substantial opposition.

Consider the following list of the great range of public programs which are shared between governments:

<u>EDUCATION</u>

Strengthening educational administration
Facilities, equipment, renovation
Teacher training
Library resources

Vocational/adult education
Special programs for handicapped, disadvantaged children, migrants
Grants to associated non-profit organizations

HEALTH

Medicaid
Medicare
Social Security
Aid for the disadvantaged
Unemployment compensation
Aid for the handicapped

WELFARE

Supplemental Nutritional Assistance Program (SNAP, formerly Food
    Stamp Program
Aid to Families with Dependent Children (AFDC)
Housing assistance
Tax exemption and subsidy
Handicapped programs
Social Security and retirement assistance

WORKFORCE

Workforce training assistance
Labor protection laws
Employment services
Youth Corps and youth employment assistance

RURAL LIFE

Agricultural crop assistance and subsidies
Subsidies for fertilizers, pesticides, insecticides
Subsidies for land development and protection
Loans and loan guarantees at subsidy rates
Rural school assistance
Programs to spread communications systems and cpmputers

State administrative expenses

Rural community development; Extension services, community facilities, family assistance, farm income supplements, marketing assistance, foreign sales assistance, forestry and land conservation.

LAW ENFORCEMENT

Law Enforcement Assistance Administration
Grants for law enforcement equipment and facilities
Grants to improve law enforcement skills
Open discretionary grants.

TRANSPORTATION

Aviation: planning grants, general aviation assistance, Airports and Airways Trust Fund

Highways: the Highway Trust Fund, funds for primary highways, fund for secondary roads, urban extensions, rural routes, bridges, tranportation safety, beautification.

PUBLIC FACILITIES

Power plants
Power distribution systems
Water system development
River/lake development and water conservation
Water distribution systems
Airports
Water ports
Public land development
Communications

THE LEGAL ESTABLISHSMENT

Definition of what is legal and illegal
Civil rights, race, gender equity issues
Definition of taxing authority
Definition of the authority to regulate – many issues

Definition of the range of legal discretion

Regulation of private sector practices

ENERGY

Mining and minerals extraction

Oil extraction, fracking

Gas, oil transmission

Power generation

Power transmission and distribution

Solar/wind power

Water power

Energy regulation, taxation and safety protection

THE MODERATE PARTY AGENDA

1. Concentrate authority where possible at the state/local government level. Sharing power promotes democracy because it is easier for citizens and organizations to reach and influence local governments. Especially with social services programs, most national governments are seen as remote and preoccupied with broader issues. Decentralization also enhances the total cadre of public leadership.

2. Aid and support local governments in achieving higher public service effectiveness and responsiveness, and of creating a better and more capable public service. In general, local administration of public programs is seen as more practical and less theoretical or doctrinaire. Program success is more likely to be evaluated in terms of how well the public is served.

3. Deliberately take power out of the hands of centrist elites, reduce elitist collusion and the power of centrist government organizations, and reduce the range of public activities that are vulnerable to corrupt control. It also importantly shifts the attention of special interest lobbying groups from a single target to a variety of governments, more attuned to the general public interest.

4. Build the most collaborative relationships between the central government and local governments. Regional governments have roles to play which are genuinely regional in nature – for example, regional road nets, the allocation of land uses, the provision of public utilities or the priorities between conflicting demands on government.

BALANCED INTERNATIONAL RELATIONSHIPS

To begin with, the Moderate Party would establish its resistance to widespread demands that the US be "the policeman of the world", "the banker of the world", and the "social services provider for the world". The sum of these demands for U. S. "responsibility" are truly overwhelming. They would demand a compelling obligation with respect to the following countries: Afghanistan, Pakistan, Iraq, Yemen, the Philippines, Puerto Rico, Saudi Arabia, Sudan and South Sudan, Syria, Libya, Ethiopia, Eritrea, Nigeria, Cuba, Haiti, the Gaza Strip, Honduras, Venezuela, El Salvador, Guatamala, and the Dominican Republic. In addition, the U. S. is expected to maintain a whole series of highly important and often prickly relationships with world powers: China, Russia, India, Japan, Mexico, Canada, Vietnam, S. Korea, Egypt, Turkey and Israel. Finally, there is a whole wonderful set of relationships with our long term friends and allies.

The key Moderate Party position should be to support efforts at negotiation and conflict resolution whenever it is possible, to help other countries to solve their own problems, but at the same time, the U. S. should stay out of direct participation in the internal affairs of other countries. Countries can and do resolve their own conflicts, as the recent agreement between the leaders of Ethiopia and Eritrea seems to show, and previous examples are Colombia, Vietnam, and the brave people of Sudan.

There has seldom been a time in world history where the crises have been so frequent and ominous. It has been estimated that there are 38 million internally displaced persons plus another 31 million people as refugees. 28

OECD countries have spent up to $25 billion per year in more than 20 countries. Huge refugee camps exist in a number of African and Middle Eastern countries. Of the top 20, 11 are in MENA and Africa.

The United Nations has developed a widespread institutional base of organizations designed to deal with the great difficulties of life in a third of the countries of the world. Look at the range of UN organizations:

- The Food and Agriculture Organization
- World Health Organization.
- The International Atomic Energy Agency
- International Civil Aviation Organization
- The International Fund for Agricultural Development
- The International Labor Organization
- The International Maritime Organization
- International Monetary Fund
- International Telecommunications Organization
- The United Nations High Commissioner for Refugees
- UNICEF
- UNESCO
- UN Industrial Development Organization
- UN Economic, Scientific and Culture Organization
- International Bank for Reconstruction and Development
- International Development Association
- Center for Settlement of Investment Disputes
- International Finance Corporation
- Multi-lateral Investment Center.

But it also true that it is easier to provide aid to victims that it is to deal with the causes of these human threats. It is easier still just to utter bland assurances of intended accomplishment. Thus, there is some truth in the Trump concern that international organizations deal more with the treatment than the cure, and the concern that, in its participation in international relationships and programs, the US has been "suckered." into carrying more than its fair share of the cost and burden.

There then is the concern that international institutions and programs have become too centrist, bureaucratic and tending to act like a version of State Socialism, and the feeling that too much of what emanates from international organizations is merely useless blather. Consider, for example, the membership of the UN Human Rights Council. It contains some of the most blatant violators of human rights in the world: China, Cuba, Burundi, Afghanistan, Angola, Congo, Egypt, Ethiopia, Iraq, Qatar, Rwanda, Saudi Arabia, United Arab Emirates, Venezuela, and of course, Russia. Former U. S. ambassador to the UN, Nikki Haley, called the council "a protector of human-rights abuses and a cesspool of political bias."

But: a lot of programs have really proved to be highly valuable. Financial services such as the World Bank, the IMF, the African unit, the Asian unit, and organizations like the World Food Fund are successful. There have been extensive peacekeeping missions in India/Pakistan, Haiti, Mali, W. Sahara, Darfur in Sudan, Liberia, Cote d'Ivoire, CAR, DRC, Cyprus, Lebanon, Egypt/Israel, and most recently, Syria, where the UN and individual nations are providing aid for more than 2 million people in a country of 17 million. Consider the range and breadth of the interventions of world organizations in conflicts around the world

Afghanistan	Chad
Azerbaijan	Cyprus*
Bosnia	E. Timor
Burundi	Ethiopia
Cambodia	Cote D'Ivoire*
Central African Republic	Democratic Republic of Congo*
Gaza	Serbia
Greece	Syria*
Haiti*	Democratic Republic of Congo
India/Pakistan*	Sierra Leone
Israel/Gaza/ Egypt*	S. Sudan*
N. Korea	Sri Lanka
Kuwait	Syria
Liberia	Timor-Leste
Lebanon*	Uzbekistan
Mali*	W. Sahara*
Myanmar	Yemen (31)
Rwanda	

One of the world's most serious problems is perceived to be that of Iran. The "problem" of Iran is really two problems. The first is the threat that Iran really plans to develop – and use – nuclear weapons on one or more unspecified enemies, and it is therefore a serious need for the world community to somehow prevent such a catastrophe. Beyond nuclear weapons however, there is an even more serious problem of Iran's extensive and continuing support of terrorism all over the world. Under President Trump, the U. S. finally strengthened its policy stance to press Iran about its support of terrorism, and this in turn is seen as putting new pressure on the religious leadership, and also on the standard and more moderate formal government. The Iranian people are increasingly questioning their government's policies and actions, along with older and surging outrage over government corruption, internal civic conflict, lack of adequate social services, rampant drug addiction, government mismanagement, the secret and suspect role of the Iranian Revolutionary Guard Corps (IRGC), and some of the economic controls exercised by the mosques. But there is a serious dislike of the U. S. and the government is gradually strengthening its ties to Russia and China. Iran has turned toward Europe to keep the nuclear agreement intact, and to promote investment, especially for its small businesses. It wants to get Europe to shelter Iranian earnings from the sale of gas and oil. At this point, it would appear that the Moderate Party should concentrate on the more extensive and destructive threats of Iran's support for terror around the world.

And then there is "The North Korea Problem". In addition to the atomic bomb/ballistic missile problem, N. Korea has a more than 400,000 man standing army, plus organized reserves of about 1.5 million. It also has "thousands" of long-range artillery pieces, aircraft, ships, etc.; in other words, one of the largest military establishments in the world. It is said to have a stockpile of nerve agents; it has had serious military contacts with and support of Syria, Lebanon, Iran, and other oppressive regimes. The North Korean government is, ominously, a harsh military dictatorship capable of actually committing some horrible outrage, and it is seen as the one regime in the world that can be insane enough to precipitate a nuclear war.

Part of the North Korea problem is that the whole population is very brain washed, and there is little realistic hope that some effective resistance to the present regime could be formed. Children are all regimented and brain washed. Oppressive government sanctions are said to have contributed to malnutrition, energy shortages, lack of consumer goods, equipment maintenance, and any pretense of trying to provide adequate public services and infrastructure. North Korean citizens are compelled to spend 6 days/ week working for the State at low wages. Many jobs are useless or of very low value, with little chance for training or promotion. Life is seriously worse outside of Pyongyang. The State Socialist regime is surely one of the most incompetent in the world. Agriculture inadequate and locked into the Middle Ages; manufacturing cannot compete on world markets. Very minor infringements can lead to punishments, and more than 120,000 people are in prison camps, held under brutal conditions. In short, this is an extraordinary government, oppressive and tyrannical, that seems widely supported by its victims, stoutly sustained and even worshiped. Per Michael Kirby, chair of the UN Commission of Inquiry on Human Rights, has stated "The gravity, scale, duration and nature of the unspeakable atrocities committed in the country reveal a totalitarian state that does not have any parallel in the contemporary world."

In another arena of the world, The United Nations Relief and Works Agency (UNRWA) has spent hundreds of millions of dollars per year on support of Palestinian people in several Mid East countries, and it has been subsidizing them for more than 70 years! It is estimated that it is now supporting more than 5.5 million people worldwide, including more than 2,000,000 in Jordan, 800,000 in the West Bank of Israel, 1.3 million in the Gaza Strip, 460,000 in Lebanon, and an estimated 500,000 still in Syria. UNRWA continues to provide housing for thousands of people, much of it in the form of huge "temporary – but permanent – camps" in many countries. It pays about $1.2 billion per year to support Palestinians in Lebanon alone. It also pays for primary education for 270 thousand children; runs health clinics, and feeds more than 1 million people regularly. Jordan has more than 2 million Palestinian refugees. Gaza does not have a real government; it is essentially run by a terrorist militia. People really live off of UNRWA and the permanent assistance of other sources, and thousands work in Israel to earn their living. And it seems difficult for Western political leadership to concede that the "government" of Gaza is simply an extended terrorist militia organization and not really a government at all. And the Gaza problem links inevitably to the Israel problem. For the Moderate Party, the policy line should be that Israel must be protected, based on a 60 year history of support, but that Israel must resist the tendency for heavy duty attacks on Gaza and to count more on negotiation and compromise, however bleak are the prospects.

But it is also necessary and important for the U. S. and the Moderate Party to face up to the false and hopeless basis for this interminable support.

Most of the world recognizes the reality that, despite their emotional hopes, there will never be a separate Palestinian State, after 70 years of specious expectations and failed negotiations. If there is never to be a Palestinian State, then there will never be any "right of return". Any policy based this false assumption is wrong and irresponsible for UNWRA to maintain. It may be difficult and distressing, but in the long run, it is wiser and more humane to help people find permanent homes in the countries where they now actually live. It is also critical to help the huge refugee camps to winnow themselves away, in part because they perpetuate inferior lives and they have become threats to their sponsoring countries. In Lebanon for example, there are serious problems of refugee camp crime, terrorist recruitment, extremist distrust, drug use and ethnic clashes. Nor is it necessarily a problem of money. The United States has reduced its funding to UNRWA, and it is argued that the US NEEDS A PLAN. Now, the US involvement is heavily military, but it is also heavily involved in social and humanitarian enterprises. The US, for example, pays about 42% of the costs of World Food Program work. Africa is not, and should not be, a US. responsibility, and in fact, China, Europe, Turkey, India, etc. are heavily involved. There is a legitimate concern with long term unreality, and the sense that the U. S. is being forced to bear on unfair share of costs. It appears that, however reluctantly, other countries are now raising their share of the agency's costs.

The Syria problem seems now not to have any rational outcome. Al-Hassad will survive, the country is in ruins, and it is supported by the wrong people. It is almost inevitable that, however the Syrian war ends, the Syria that is left will be almost destroyed, and will have to be rebuilt from the bottom up. Syria's pre-war population was about 22 million, but an estimated 5 million have fled the country, and an additional 6-10 million are internally displaced, living in temporary locations. High percentages of public services are out of commission, and/or seriously deteriorated. Who is responsible for managing and financing this rehabilitation? The obvious answer is the Syrian government, since Assad will not allow much people-based bottom up authority. Syria now has detention centers filled with thousands of people seized and controlled by the Syrian military. Almost all public services and infrastructure are destroyed or in horrible shape. Thousands of homes and businesses, and schools, and government offices have been destroyed. It must be reiterated: this is not a U. S. responsibility.

And in fact, there is a growing tendency is to say "This is a Russian thing, but they must move against Iranian domination." In fact, the Syria that survives the war will be a basket case, and a drag on any ally, and it is hard to see Russia rushing in with lots of aid. And much of the perceptions remain that "The war is not yet over". The likelihood is that Iran will be stuck with the world position that it's shares much of the blame for the Syrian debacle, and thus should make major efforts to restore the country. It is doubtful whether they will, and Syria in crippled condition, is a problem from which nobody gains, and everybody hopes to abandon.

Another country in deep trouble is Cambodia. The Prime Minister is acting as a real tyrant, using the police an army to assault, intimidate, arrest, imprison without due process. Also, the government has closed down newspapers and TV stations, and all of the other elements of tyranny. As usual, the cry has been raised: "What it the United States going to do to solve this problem?" As usual, proposals include import/export prohibitions, ending aid to their military, sanctions on individuals.

Or take the case of Zimbabwe. It was argued that once long-time President Robert Mugabe was out, the country would straighten itself out. But the new President, Emmerson Mnangagwa, seems increasingly like Mugabe revisited. There is a bitter joke in the country about his "CIBD" program: meaning, coercion, intimidation, beatings, and displacement." The government is still seen as "a patronage machine."

But without doubt, the most important and confusing international relationship for the American government and indeed for the American people is undoubtedly the relationship with the Republic of China. China itself has gone through remarkable changes which have to be understood before one can begin to scope out a workable relationship. As early as the mid 1970's, the Communist government of the People's Republic of China began to recognize that the state socialist economy was not capable of expanding fast enough to keep up with a growing population, and that, while the agricultural sector of the economy could be improved sufficiently to feed this growing population, agriculture was never going to be more than a subsistence sector and could not generate enough spare economic value to finance the development of other sectors of the economy.

As the Chinese economy blossomed, speculation began about the government. Very reluctantly, and after much debate and political infighting, the ruling Chinese Communist Party (CCP) was forced to recognize that a shift to a market-based economy was absolutely necessary even though it abandoned many of the sacred principles and practices of the politically centralized command and control economic system. The CCP attempted to retreat as little as possible and as slowly as it could. The private sector had to be unleashed and encouraged; but politically the government sought ways to retain crucial economic control while slowly relinquishing much ownership of productive resources. Control was to be maintained through a combination of retention by state owned enterprises of the "commanding heights" portions of the economy, continued control over the state banking system, the ownership of the land, control of the pace and shape of private sector development through regulations governing entry into business, and the nature of foreign direct investment. The CCP leadership feel that they can control the nature of changes about to occur, and to sell to the population the idea that prosperity was the product of a modified version of the old state socialism.

What seems to have emerged is pathological governance. Their pathologies include an almost uncontrolled expansion of corruption of the political leadership from top to bottom, peddling of money and influence between the public and the private sectors, a tendency to try to hang on to failed state owned enterprises despite their economic failure, a general neglect of public goods and services, and the accumulation of huge public debt, making the Chinese government the most heavily indebted in the world. China has deliberately failed to fund social services in order to spend the money on economic priorities which still means breakneck urbanization, overdevelopment in manufacturing, excessive dependence on exports, expanded coal fired electrical generation capacity, heavy metals dumped into the air, and nasty chemicals dumped into the water. Water sources are extremely inadequate and yet they are recklessly dissipated. All of these problems are known. The real issue is whether the Communist Party can change itself enough to cope with them, and then whether they have the skills to do so.

But the key to the whole structure of the Chinese economy is the unprecedented percentage of the national economy that is captured and controlled and deployed by the government, taking wealth away from almost all organizations in the country and from hundreds of millions of individuals. Even the growing middle class of the country is essentially an elite that benefits from this massive government usurpation of wealth, government subsidy, heavy preferment; even some monopolies. When the CCP undertook a program to reduce the number and reach of SOEs, what was often done was to group many smaller SOEs under a massive holding company. Thus, the number of SOEs was touted as vastly reduced, but ---.

It is this vast, complex, confusing, and horribly decadent Chinese government with which the U. S. government and private businesses must deal, and that government still maintains all or most of the key elements of control:

Limits on the % of foreign investment in Chinese enterprises.

Deliberate purchase of American technology ownership including the purchase of companies; deliberate forcing of technology transfers from American firms doing business in China.

Almost total ownership of land; regulatory control of buildings on the land, especially by local governments.

Control over the granting of licenses of hundreds of types.

Limits on market size permitted to private companies

Favoritism in labor relations; labor unions made instruments of the government.

Government price controls. Despite recent drawbacks, the government still controls vital segments of the economy.

Prejudicial and highly suspect government contract relationships

Official corruption; national and local governments. Much "selective" enforcement of the hundreds of thousands of regulations.

Import substitution policies, and massive control and regulation of both imports and exports, always favoring Chinese organizations, many of them SOEs.

Banking system control, again strongly biases in favor of SOEs.

China and human rights. The government will not tolerate any protest against it's human rights failures, and foreign firms are not excluded.

The U. S. cannot negotiate trade agreements or anything else with the Chinese government in any straight-forward, normal manner. It will always come up to massive, often secretive and always confusing barriers that make little sense in Western terms, but are imperative in Chinese terms. But in a sense, if somehow these negotiations result in moving the Chinese government, however reluctantly, in the right directions, the Moderate Party must recognize this and cater to it. It is important that we see China not in limited terms of economic competition, but in terms of a fully developed and highly sophisticated state which has matured in very broad terms.

Venezuela is a country in mortal danger. A country of 29 million, it is in serious trouble in every possible way, and again critics are asking "what is the United States going to do to solve this problem?" The leadership has been socialist and populist and is described as distorted and "economically illiterate". The economy will have shrunk by 50% since just 2014, post Chavez. Inflation is officially 13%, but is actually much worse, now being estimated by external analysis at more than 14,000%, with far worse to some, and very soon. A pound of chicken now may cost something like 2.1 million of the official bolivares. What should be the responsibility of the U. S. in Venezuela? Never help or encourage the horrible socialist government at the top; try to help the people themselves from the bottom up.

Many normal items in the civilian economy are scarce or non-existent, especially food and medicines. Oil production, which is the key to the economy, is down, in part by a stupid lack of maintenance and repair. The currency is almost worthless, and the government skews prices, destroying parts of the economy in the process. Skilled people are fleeing the country, and others are leaving government jobs because of the very low pay. It has been estimated that, in a country having about 29 million, more than 3.8 million have fled the country, including 2 million in 2018. The Moderate Party would be well justified to maintain support of the anti-Maduro designated government, and leading a world-wide effort not just to oppose, but to find ways to help and assist.

Hamas, located in the Gaza Strip is locked in implacable conflict with Israel, and in fact with the competing Muslim interests operating from Israel. There is a long-standing complaint against the Israeli blockade, but in fact, it has been in place for more than 70 years. The Hamas regime is not really a government; it is a militia force. Much of the costs of governance and social services have been borne by Fattah or international donors. The Moderate Party should recognize that Hamas is incapable of functioning as a real government and it brings its resident victims only misery and despair.

As an example of the frustrations of dealing with regimes, U. S. efforts to produce a good outcome in Iraq are frustrated by the Iraqis themselves. They have produced a succession of bumbling incompetent, unpopular governments. Those governments have failed to deal with terrorist rebels in the country. The economy has never really been rehabilitated, there are chronic shortages of water, electricity, medical services, schools, etc. There continue to be serious conflict along the ancient lines of Sunni vs. Shia. The government is widely and bitterly condemned for its universal corruption, and the rigging of elections – which tend to be contests between different groups of tyrants and fools. And outside meddling both U. S. and Iranian meddling. The old saw: "Government is not the answer; government is the problem."

Unfortunately, this list of critical country problems can go on and on. Previous assessments by the author list 106 countries in the world are in some form of serious trouble, defined as wars, insurrections, rebellions heavy government oppression and wide civilian outrage against it, and massive government incompetence, waste and mismanagement, and universal corruption in every possible form. The population of Africa is exploding. By 2050 it will have 25% of the world's population, and it will accelerate and grow more complex and far more difficult to control. It is hoped that, by 2030, 43% of the population will be "middle class" and far more stable and productive, but right now, Africa is already overwhelmed, with bad governments, weak economies, horrible conflicts, high poverty levels, lack of infrastructure, lack of social services, lack of freedom.

THE MODERATE PARTY AGENDA

1. The role of the Moderate Party is first and foremost to remain firmly locked in reality. The international arena is now characterized by zealous overcommitment and policies driven all to often by fear and cowardice and hysteria.

2. The apparatus of international organizations is far too complex, far too pompous, vastly overgrown, and intensely bureaucratic. Americans also strongly feel that the U. S. has been burdened with far too great a part of the support and financing of international matters.

3. The Party should stoutly maintain its insistence that the U. S. should not try to be "the policeman of the world', or "the banker of the world, or "the social service provider of the world."

4. As much as possible, the U. S. should insist that other nations handle their own affairs, with the U. S. deliberately limited to roles of negotiation and perhaps refereeing.

5. There should be a very strong backing for the valuable UN work for aid and assistance in foreign countries but the key is also to aid people and not oppressors. The U. S. would be responsible only for its "fair share".

6. Iran must be treated as two problems. It is capable at some point of creating nuclear weapons and the missiles to deliver them. The issue

is whether they will really want to do so, and whether their leadership would ever make the fatal mistake of trying to use them. The betting should be that, in the last analysis, they will never be used.

7. The second Iran problem is their broad and deliberate support and encouragement of terrorist organizations all over the world. Iran is the worst supporter of terrorism, and the U. S. and the rest of the world should be implacable foes of this tyranny.

8. Much the same could be said about North Korea. It too is capable of developing nuclear weapons and delivery systems. In addition, it has one of the largest and most ominous standing military establishments in the world. The best that the U. S. and the rest of the world can do is to watch and guard, and hope that the N. Korean leader is not as insane and irrational as he appears.

9. There is a valid case to realize that there will never be a Palestinian State after almost 80 years of yearning, and that it is time to work to allow Palestinians to become full residents in the countries in which they now live. At the same time, it should be recognized that Hamas is never going to be the base for a Palestinian State, and it is simply a horrible terrorist militia group. The People of Gaza deserve some form of help to break free of this terror and form some kind of legitimate government.

10. There are other problems: Venezuela, Zimbabwe, Algeria, Libya, Sudan, Syria, Cambodia, etc. The fact that there has been and will forever be some horrible problems being played out simply reinforces the need for the U. S. to protect its own interests first and foremost.

11. Finally, the ultimate and by far the most significant relationship in the world is now that with China. Any U. S. government, and every element of the American economy will have to settle into a new and extraordinarily complex and sophisticated relationship with China, much like we have long maintained with Europe. China should not be treated as a "problem"; it must be understood as a new and long term relationship that should be seen as collaborative cooperative, and ultimately supportive.

SUMMARY

At the core of the intent and purpose of a proposed new Moderate Party is to restore the balance between political parties and the American people. The two parties see their status as superior to the wellbeing of our citizens, and they think that people must see themselves identified by their political party affiliation. Let it be understood: the Moderate Party would demand that the lives and advancement of individual people is far more important than that of any political party.

The intent of any government is to improve the state of American citizens. It is more important for the government to perform well than it is for political parties to perform well. The importance of the government –President, Congress, the courts -is to advance its success as a government, not as the base for party activities. It is more important for the President to serve the people, and not to serve some political party agenda. It is more important for the Congress to function effectively by law and regulation than to serve as the base for contending political parties.

The real world is not about political oversight or philosophy. It is about the people being human, and being able to count on the government and the country to help them do so. The Moderate Party must not fall into the trap of believing that life lies in political policy and maneuver. It lies in the capacity for people to live their lives within the framework of American culture, of which politics is one element.

The people have every right to have a government that is responsive and effective and not on its affinity for cheap politics. Good governance is not to be defined as maximum government, but on the provision of real and necessary government. That is why there needs to be a serious change, through the Moderate Party, away from the ominous power of special interest politics. One of the core purposes of the Party is to reverse the long term trend to give way to the powers and demands of these hundreds of special interests, exercised all up and down the structures of government. Such special interests represent a disturbing pattern for deciding the affairs of government, cast against the general interests of the whole population. They become embedded in law or regulation and the system locks them in "forever, and many have become the ideal vehicle for favoritism, preferment, corruption, waste and obsolescence.

The true heart of the Moderate Party must be the values by which our citizens really live – our sense of humanity, the real desire for the capacity of self-reliance, our honesty and integrity. The business of governing should be based on a strong sense of responsibility for our acts, and a willingness to be accountable to the American public for those acts. We have learned that we must constantly be aware of what it takes to produce and maintain a true equality and this requires that we never attempt to pit one element of American society against another, especially for cheap, shoddy political advantage. Finally, the philosophy of American moderate governance will remind us once again to avoid the colossal mistakes of State Socialism which have tortured many of the other countries of the world.

One of the problems to be faced by the Moderate Party is the nature of our politics. In addition to the impingement of special interest politics, the Party should commit itself to bring governance at all levels to a more rational level of coherence, simplicity, effectiveness and relevance. There should be a commitment to avoiding the condition of a national government that sees itself as dominant, all-powerful, and overly demanding. There will always be a whole range of very complex and sophisticated relationships between the government and the private sector, and this would be healthy and productive. The essence of policy should be not to oppose and control, but to collaborate and cooperate.

Similarly, it is probably time to reexamine the whole range of relationships between the central national government and local governments at the state, county, and urban levels, and in the program networks across all government operating functions. The key should be the generally recognized reality that operational government is almost always best pursued at the local government level.

The federal government must concentrate itself on two of its most important and formidable sources of power: the power to tax and the power to regulate. In both arenas, the great concern has tended to become the gradual and ominous broadening and deepening of the power to control. It is deeply disturbing to believe that the structure of taxation has fallen increasingly into the hands of the politics of special interests. It is equally disturbing to recognize that the hundreds of thousands of pages of regulations and implementing procedures has passed beyond comprehension and rationality, and to fear that government regulatory enforcement is increasingly seen as real oppression. The greater the range of regulation, the greater has become the potentials for corruption in the form of fraud, waste, abuse, an bumbling mismanagement.

And these enormous excesses are terribly expensive. The Moderate Party would create highly desirable improvements in government performance if it can cut out the low value elements of tax and regulatory expenditures, get rid of the trash, the obsolete, the pointless and the ineffective. We must stop approving "everything", and start learning set priorities. Again, the policy should concentrate on support, assistance, and protection, and not on opposition, prevention, resistance, and punishment.

The other great arena of governance is that of the relationships between the U. S., other nations and international organizations. After WW II, the earnest world turned very international. New institutions were invented like the UN, the World Bank, ASEAN, and NATO. Convulsions produced a new Soviet Union, China, North Korea, Vietnam and Cambodia. World political leadership turned not to representative democracy but to various forms of State Socialism. A tide of newly liberated governments produced not excellence but top down centrist elites, many of them oppressive and incompetent. The new international institutions have been a fascinating blend of real assistance in the affairs of governance, plus a lot of overbearing bumbling.

There is not single overarching policy framework that can guide and direct American affairs in this complex international arena. What is needed is a careful, realistic, and non-hysterical program of long term relationships dealing collaboratively with a group of good and productive national relationships, and with common sense and courage against those that are enemies and oppressive. China can no longer be seen either as an economic competitor or business partner. It is now very broad, far-reaching and fully mature major element of the world, and it must be understood in this long-term and enduring sense.

There are three far more problematic international relationships that must be treated with great care. They are North Korea, Iran and Venezuela. It would be a mistake for the U. S. to believe that it is somehow responsible for "solving" these international dilemmas and mitigating their influence. The Moderate Party must sturdily resist the constant imprecations for the U.

S. to become "the police man of the word", or 'the banker of the world", or "the social services provider of the world". We can and should be the constant force for collaboration, cooperation, improvement and support – along with moderation, common sense and courage.

SOURCES

Country Reports on Terrorism, U. S. Department of State November 2009.

Corruption Perceptions Index 2012, Transparency International

Most Dangerously Polluted Cities, All Countries.org. 2011.

Inequality-adjusted Human Development Index, Human Development Report, 2010.

"A Haven for Malcontents", Economist, July 13, 2013, p. 4

"The World's Ten Most Authoritarian Leaders", World Policy Journal, Fall, 2012.

"Miserable and Weak Again", Economist, Nov. 16, 2013.

Pavlak, Alex. Dr., "The Future of Energy Initiative, state of Maryland Future of Energy Initative, 2018'

Cruz, Jose Miguel, "MS-13", Washington Post, Jan. 1, 1018.

Richardson, Elliot, "Reflections of a Radical Moderate", Pantheon Books, 1996.

McFaul, Michael, "From Cold War to Hot Peace", Houghton Mifflin, 2018.

Sliver, Charles, and Hyman, David A., "Overcharged: Why Americans Pay Too Much for Health Care", CATO Institute, Washington 2018.

Judt, Tony, "Ill Falls the Land", Penguin Press, N. Y. 2010.

Sproul, R. C., "Essential Truths of the Christian Faith", Tyndale House Publishing, Carol Stream, Il. 1992.

Goklany, Indur M., "Improving the State of the World", CATO Institute, Washington, D. C., 2007.

Tommelli, Pier Angelo, "The Rise and Fall of State Owned Enterprise in the Western World", Cambridge U. Press, 2000.

Willits, Peter, "Non-Government Organizations in World Politics", Routledge, London, 2011.

Bahadur, Jay, "Deadly Waters", People Books, N. Y. 2011

Nelson, Joan, "Reforming Health and Education", Overseas Development Council, Washington, D. C., 1999.

Zupan, Mark A. "Inside Job: How Government Insiders Suborn the Public Interest", Cambridge U. Press, 2017.

Edwards, Chris, "Downsizing the Federal Government", CATO Institute, Washington, D. C.,2005.

Howard, Philip K., "The Rule of Nobody", Norton, N. Y. 2014.

Victor, Halts, Thurber, Editors; "Oil and Governance", Cambridge U. Press, 2004.

Singh, Kiklal Pol, "Black is a Country", Harvard U. Press, 2004.

Economy, Elizabeth C., "The River Runs Black", Council on Foreign Relations, Cornell U. Press, Ithaca, 2004.

Keynes, John Maynard, "The General Theory of Employment, Industry and Money", Harvard U. Press 1964.

Ginsberg, Benjamin, and Crenson, Mathew, 'Downsizing Democracy", Johns Hopkins U. Press, Baltimore, 2002.

Kahli, Atul, "State Directed Development", Cambridge U. Press 2004.

Brice, Robert, "Smaller, Faster, Lighter, Denser, Cheaper" Public Affairs Press, N. Y., 2010.

Rogers, Peter and Leal, Susan, "Running Out of Water", Palgrave, N.Y. 2010.

Pearce, Fred, "When the Rivers Run Dry", Beacon Press, Boston, 2006.

Luce, Edward, "Time to Start Thinking", Grove Press, N. Y. 2012

Glozer, Ken G., "Corn Ethanol: Who Pays? Who Benefits?", Hoover Institute Press, Stanford, Cal., 2011.

United States Department of State: National Consortium for the Study of Terrorism and Responses to Terrorism: Annex of Statistical Information, Country Reports on Terrorism, 2012.

"Nasty Neighbourhood", Economist, Aug. 2, 2014, p. 41.

World Development Indicators, "Poverty", 2004.

Chandler, Michael, and Gunaratria, Rohan, "Countering Terrorism: Reaktion Books, 2007.

Lankford, James, Senator. "Federal Fumbles", U. S. Government, U.S. Senate publications, Volumes One and Two.

Diner, Dan, "Lost in the Sacred", Princeton U. Press, 2009.

Boston, Andrew G., Ed., "The Legacy of Jihad", New York, Prometheus Books, 2005.

Ayittey, George B. N., "Africa in Chaos", St. Martins Press, 1998.

Rotberg, Robert, Ed., "When States Fail: Causes and Consequences", Princeton U. Press, 2004.

Kuran, Timur, "The Long Divergence", Princeton U. Press, 2011.

Bueno De Mesquita, Bruce, and Smith, Alistair, "The Dictator's Handbook", Public Affairs, 2011.

Bhagwati, Jagdish, "Free Trade Today", Princeton U. Press, 2002.

Honenkamp Herbert, "Principles of Antitrust", West Academic, 2017

Hayek, F. A. "The Fatal Conceit: The Errors of Socialism", U. of Chicago Press, 1988

Yergin, Daniel, and Stanislaw, Joseph, "The Commanding Heights", Simon and Schuster, 1998.

Bingman, Charles F., "Governance from the Bottom Up", iUniverse Publishers, 2016.

Bingman, Charles F., "Governments From Hell", iUniverse Publishers, 2015.

Bingman, Charles F., "Governments in the Muslim World", iUniverse Publishers, 2013.

Bingman, Charles F., "Changing Governments in India and China", IUniverse Publishers, 2016, (Reissue by new printer).

Bingman, Charles F., "Reforming China's Government", Xlibris Press, 2010.

Bingman, Charles, F. "Why Governments Go Wrong", iUniverse Publishers, 2006.

Freedom House: "Freedom Country Rankings 2011 – Country Rankings

The World Fact Book: "The World's Most Populous Cities, Metropolitan Areas and Urban Agglomerations, 2008.

List of United Nations Peacekeeping Missions, 2015.

NUMBEO: "Quality of Life Index for 2012.

UNHCR: "Facts and Figures on Refugees", 2015.

Washington Post, July 26, 2015, "Troubles at electric utility signal depth of Puerto Rico's crisis".

UNDP 2005: "Close to 43 million people worldwide are displaced because of conflict and persecution."

AllCountries.org: "Most Dangerously Polluted Cities", 2004.

Rotberg, Robert I., "Failed States in a World of Terror", Foreign Affairs Journal, July/August 2002.

Bhagwati, Jagdish, "Free Trade Today", Princeton U. Press, 2002.

Andrusz Gregory, Harloe, Michael, "Cities After Socialism", Oxford, Blackwell Publishers, 1996.

Bingman, Charles F. "China Struggles to Reform", Washington Institute of China Studies, Spring, 2006.

Hayek, F. A., "The Fatal Conceit: The Errors of Socialism", U. of Chicago Press, 1988.

Isbister, John, "Promises Not Kept", Hartford, Conn., Kumarian Press, 1993.

"Making Sense of Subsidiarity", The Center for Economic Policy Research, London, 1993.

O'Donnell, Guillermo, and Shmitter, Phillipe, "Transitions from Authoritarian Rule", the Johns Hopkins U. Press, 1986.

Shleifer, Andrei, Vishny, Robert W., "The Grabbing Hand: Government Pathologies and Their Cures", Harvard U. Press, 1998.

Waterbury, John, "Exposed to Innumerable Delusions", London, Cambridge U. Press, 1993.

Kohli, Atul, "State-Directed Development", Cambridge U. Press, 2004.

Michalski, Mark M., "Trade and Procurement Reform in Poland and China: Responding to the Next Globalization Wave of Interdependent Economies", Journal of the Washington Institute of China Studies, Fall, 2010.

The United Nations Convention Against Corruption, Dec.2003. The UN Declaration Against Corruption and Bribery, 1996.

The Globalist: "A (Very) Brief History of Corruption", Jul. 1, 2012.

Economist: "Bribery: Graft Work", Dec. 6, 2014.

Transparency International: Corruptions Perceptions Index, 2015.

Transparency International: Bribepayers Index, 2011.

Economist: "Corruption and Natural Resources: A Fight for Light", Oct. 24, 2015.

World Health Organization (WHO), "Health Performance Rank by Country", 2011.

The Guardian: "World Educational Rankings: Which Country Does Best at Reading, Maths, Science? Datablog, 2015.

Most Dangerously Polluted Cities, AllCountries.org, 2011.

Detter, Dag, and Folster, Stefan, "The Public Wealth of Nations: How Management of Public Assets Can Boost or Bust Economic Growth", New York, Palgrave McMillan, 2015.

Lomborg, Bjorn, "The Skeptical Environmentalist" Cambridge U. Press, 2001.

Economist: "Water Consumption: A Canal Too Far", Sep. 17, 2014.

World Development Indicators: "Assessing Vulnerability", 2004.

World Development Indicators: "Enhancing Security", 2004.

Carter, Ashton B., Perry, William J., "Preventative Defense: A New Security Strategy for America", Washington, D. C. Brookings Institution, 1999.

Cooper, Philip J., "Government by Contract", Washington, D. C., CQ Press, 2003.

Diamond, Jared, "Collapse: How Societies Choose to Fail or Succeed", New York, Penguin Press, 2005.

Drucker, Peter F. "Managing in the Next Society", New York, St. Martins Press, 2002.

Esterbrook, Gregg, "The Progress Paradox", New York, Random House Press, 2003.

Economist Magazine – all issues for 20 years.

International Labor Office, "The Future of Urban Employment", Geneva, 1998.

Ginsberg, Benjamin, Crenson, Matthew A., "Downsizing Democracy", Baltimore, Johns Hopkins U. Press, 2002.

Klitzaard, Robert, Maclean-Aberoa, Ronald, Parris, H. Lindsay, "Corrupt Cities", Washington, D. C., World Bank Institute, 2000.

Marquette, Heather, "Corruption, Politics and Development: The Role of the World Bank", New York, Palgrave, 2003.

Moran, Theodore H., "Foreign Direct Investment and Development", Washington, D. C., The Institute for International Economics, 1999.

OECD, "Regulatory Reform in the Global Economy", Washington, D. C., 1998.

World Bank: "Extending Women's Participation in Economic Development", Washington, D. C., 2003.

Posner, Richard A. "Antitrust Law: An Economic Perspective", U. of Chicago Press, 1976.

INDEX

ABOUT THE AUTHOR

Charles F. Bingman had a thirty-year career as a U. S. Federal government manager and executive with service in the Atomic Energy Commission, the National Aeronautics and Space Administration, the Department of Transportation, and the Office of Management and Budget in the Executive Office of the President.

After retirement, he began a second career of teaching and consulting. He taught public management at the George Washington University in Washington, D. C., and as a Fellow of the Center for the Study of American Government at the Johns Hopkins University Washington Center. He has published reports on the history of management responsibilities in the U. S. Office of Management and Budget, and written numerous books and articles about governance in the United States and in numerous governments around the world.

Bingman has done consulting assignments with various organizations in the Muslim countries of Saudi Arabia, Jordan, Egypt, and the Palestinian Authority in Gaza. He has also consulted in China, Japan, the Russian Federation, Kazakhstan, Romania, Estonia, Botswana, and other countries. He is the author of: "Japanese Government Leadership and Management"(1989); "Why Governments Go Wrong" (2006); "Reforming China's Government"(2010); and "Changing Governments in India and China"(2011), "Governments From Hell" (2015), "Governance From the Bottom Up", (2016), and "Revitalizing American Governance" (2018). Bingman is an elected Fellow of the National Academy of Public Administration, and of the Cosmos Club in Washington D. C.